NICE

FRANCE TRAVEL GUIDE

2024

Practical Tips And Pointers to Know Before Visiting Nice.

Taylor Allen

All rights reserved. No part of this book may be reproduced, stored in a retrieval system, or transmitted in any form or by any means, electronic, mechanical, photocopying, recording, or otherwise, without the prior written permission of the copyright owner. The information contained in this book is for general information purposes only. The author and publisher make no representations or warranties of any kind, express or implied, about the completeness, accuracy, reliability, suitability or availability with respect to the book or the information, products, services, or related graphics contained in the book for any purpose. Any reliance you place on such information is therefore strictly at your own risk.

Copyright © 2023 by Taylor Allen.

TABLE OF CONTENT

I. Introduction _____ 7
    A. Welcome to Nice _____ 7
    B. Why Visit Nice in 2024_____ 8
    C. Quick Overview of Nice _____ 11

II. Getting There _____ 15
    A. Transportation Options_____ 15
    B. Navigating the City _____ 18

*III. Accommodations*_____ 19

IV. Exploring Nice _____ 33
    A. Must-Visit Attractions _____ 33
    B. Museums and Galleries _____ 47
    C. Day Trips from Nice _____ 53

*V. Dining and Culinary Delights*_____ 59
    A. Local Cuisine _____ 59
    B. Restaurants and Cafés _____ 66

VI. Shopping in Nice _____ 74
    A. Markets and Bazaars_____ 74
    B. Fashion and Souvenirs_____ 77

VII. Entertainment and Nightlife _____ 81
    A. Evening Activities _____ 81
    Bars and Nightclubs _____ 85

VIII. Practical Information _____ 92
    Currency and Money Matters _____ 92

Language Tips	92
Safety Tips	93
Useful Apps and Resources	94
IX. Events and Festivals in 2024	**97**
A. Annual Highlights	97
X. Conclusion	**105**
Final Thoughts on Nice	105
Planning Your Next Visit	106

Important Notice Before You Continue Reading!

A unique travel experience awaits you within these pages. This travel guide to Nice has been specifically created to leave room for your imagination, creativity, and sense of adventure. You won't any images here because we firmly believe that the beauty of every discovery should be experienced firsthand, without visual filters or preconceptions. Every monument, every places, every hidden corners awaits you with surprise and wonder, ready to enchant you when you personally reach them. Why should we spoil the excitement of that first glance, that feeling of awe? So get ready to embark on an unprecedented journey where the only means of transportation will be your imagination, and you will be your own guide. Let go of preconceived notions and be transported to an authentic Nice of discoveries. The magic of the journey begins now, but remember, the most beautiful images will be the ones you create with your own eyes

In Contrast to many guides, this book needs no detailed maps. Why? Because we firmly believe that the best discoveries happen when you get lost when you allow yourself to be carried by the flow of the places and embrace the uncertainty of the path. No predetermined itineraries or precise directions because we want you to explore Nice in your own way, without boundaries or restrictions. Let yourself be carried away and discover hidden treasures that you would never find on a map. Be bold, follow your instinct, and be prepared to be surprised. The magic of the journey begins now in your world without maps, where roads are created with each step, and the most incredible adventures awaits you in the folds of the unknown.

I. Introduction

Welcome to Nice

Ah, dear reader, welcome to the vibrant and enchanting city of Nice, nestled along the azure coastline of the French Riviera. As a local, I'm thrilled to be your guide, unveiling the secrets and treasures that make Nice a true jewel of the Mediterranean. There's an indescribable charm to this city that captivates every visitor, and it's my pleasure to help you navigate its streets, savor its flavors, and immerse yourself in its rich history.

Picture this: you arrive at Nice Côte d'Azur Airport, greeted by the warm embrace of the Mediterranean breeze, carrying with it the promise of an unforgettable adventure. The radiant sun, a constant companion in this part of the world, bathes the city in a golden glow. As you make your way into the heart of Nice, be prepared to be enchanted by a city that seamlessly combines old-world charm with a cosmopolitan flair.

Stroll down the famed Promenade des Anglais, a picturesque boulevard that stretches along the Baie des Anges. Lined with palm trees and iconic blue chairs, this is the perfect spot for a leisurely afternoon promenade. The azure waters of the Mediterranean gently lap at the pebbled shores, inviting you to dip your toes into the refreshing sea.

To truly grasp the essence of Nice, immerse yourself in the narrow, labyrinthine streets of Old Town, or Vieux Nice as the locals affectionately call it. Here, the ochre-hued buildings wear their history proudly, and every cobblestone seems to whisper tales of bygone eras. Explore hidden squares, such as the lively Place Rossetti, where you'll find the famous Fenocchio ice cream parlor, offering an array of exotic flavors that will tantalize your taste buds.

As you navigate the city, you'll encounter a delightful blend of Provençal traditions and cosmopolitan influences. Nice is a cultural mosaic, evident in its architecture, cuisine, and language. The Nicois dialect, a melodic fusion of French and Italian, is spoken with a musical cadence that adds to the city's unique identity.

But, my friend, let's not forget the panoramic views from Castle Hill. Ascend the winding pathways or take the elevator for a breathtaking panorama that encapsulates the beauty of Nice. As the sun sets over the Mediterranean, casting hues of pink and gold across the sky, you'll understand why artists like Matisse and Chagall found inspiration in these landscapes.

In this introduction to Nice, I urge you to let go of any preconceived notions and embrace the city's laid-back allure. Take the time to savor a café au lait in a quaint boulangerie, exchange pleasantries with locals in the markets, and relish the vibrant colors of the flower market at Cours Saleya. Nice is not just a destination; it's a sensory experience that invites you to slow down and appreciate the beauty of life.

So, my fellow traveler, as you embark on this journey through the sun-kissed streets of Nice, let curiosity be your guide, and may the Mediterranean whispers guide you to the hidden gems that await. Nice is more than a destination; it's an invitation to embrace the art of living, the French Riviera way.

Why Visit Nice in 2024

As you contemplate your travel choices for 2024, let me make a compelling case for why Nice, nestled along the sun-kissed French Riviera, should be at the top of your list.

Picture this: azure skies kissing the Mediterranean, historic cobblestone streets winding through vibrant markets, and a subtle scent of lavender lingering in the air. Nice, with its timeless elegance and lively spirit, beckons travelers with promises of enchantment and discovery.

1. The Revitalized Promenade des Anglais:

In 2024, the iconic Promenade des Anglais, the city's coastal jewel, undergoes a revitalization that enhances its allure. Stroll along this legendary promenade, framed by palm trees and overlooking the azure waters, and you'll find a perfect blend of tradition and modernity. New seating areas, artistic installations, and lively street performances now characterize this beloved stretch, creating an atmosphere where the past seamlessly intertwines with the contemporary. My advice? Grab a coffee from a nearby café, take a leisurely seat, and savor the view as the sun dips below the horizon – it's an experience that encapsulates the essence of Nice.

2. Vieux Nice's Time-Tested Charm:

Venture into the heart of Nice – the enchanting Old Town, or Vieux Nice. In 2024, this historic district remains a living testament to the city's rich cultural tapestry. The narrow cobblestone streets are lined with colorful buildings, housing quaint boutiques, artisanal shops, and bustling cafés. Dive into the vibrant Cours Saleya Market, where the scents of fresh flowers and local produce mingle, creating a sensory symphony. Make it a point to visit early in the morning to witness the market in its full glory, and perhaps indulge in a local delicacy like Socca, a chickpea-flour pancake crisped to perfection.

3. Castle Hill: A Panoramic Marvel:

Ascend Castle Hill, a verdant oasis perched above Nice, and you'll be rewarded with unrivaled panoramic views of the city and the Mediterranean beyond. In 2024, accessibility to this natural wonder has been improved, ensuring that the journey to the top is as memorable as the destination itself. Whether you choose to climb the stairs or opt for the elevator, reaching the summit unveils a vista that encapsulates the city's beauty. Pack a picnic, bask in the glow of the Riviera sun, and appreciate the timeless allure of Nice from this elevated vantage point.

4. Cultural Corners: Marc Chagall National Museum and More:

Nice isn't just about sun and sea; it's a cultural haven. In 2024, delve into the city's artistic soul by exploring its renowned museums. The Marc Chagall National Museum, a testament to the artist's profound connection with the French Riviera, unveils an extensive collection of his masterpieces. From the vibrant stained glass windows to the soul-stirring canvases, every corner resonates with Chagall's creative genius. Ensure your visit aligns with any temporary exhibitions or events for an even more immersive experience.

5. Culinary Odyssey in Nice:

2024 marks a culinary renaissance in Nice, making it a haven for food enthusiasts. Begin your gastronomic journey with a classic Niçoise Salad, expertly crafted with locally sourced ingredients. For a truly authentic experience, venture into the Old Town's hidden gems where chefs elevate traditional recipes to new heights. Seek out Chez Palmyre, a historic establishment, and let the flavors of Ratatouille dance on your palate. Engage with locals to discover the

latest culinary hotspots – Nice's culinary scene is ever-evolving, ensuring a delightful surprise with every meal.
6. Events and Festivals: A Tapestry of Celebration:

In 2024, Nice transforms into a stage for a multitude of events and festivals, each weaving a unique thread into the city's vibrant tapestry. The world-famous Nice Carnival, a spectacle of colors and creativity, enchants visitors with its grand parades and elaborate floats. Plan your visit around this time to witness the city bursting with energy. Additionally, the Nice Jazz Festival, a celebration of music that transcends genres, resonates through the streets and venues, creating an atmosphere where the soul of Nice truly comes alive.

As you ponder your travel choices for 2024, consider Nice not just as a destination but as an immersive journey into the heart of the French Riviera. The city's timeless elegance, cultural richness, and culinary delights promise an experience that transcends the ordinary. Let Nice be your canvas for creating indelible memories, where every cobblestone street and sun-drenched panorama tells a story waiting to be discovered.

Quick Overview of Nice

Let's kick off our exploration of Nice with a swift overview, like a sip of chilled rosé on the Promenade des Anglais. Nestled on the French Riviera, Nice is a captivating blend of glamour, history, and seaside charm. The azure waters of the Mediterranean greet you, and the warmth of the sun wraps you in a gentle embrace.

Inhale deeply; let the scent of fresh sea breeze and blooming flowers paint a vivid picture as we delve into the heartbeat of Nice.

1. The Promenade des Anglais: A Boulevard of Elegance and History

Our journey begins along the iconic Promenade des Anglais, a sun-kissed boulevard that stretches for miles along the Baie des Anges. Named after the English aristocracy who first strolled here in the 18th century, it is the city's pulse. Take a leisurely walk or rent a bicycle to absorb the stunning views of the Mediterranean, where the vivid hues of the sea merge seamlessly with the azure sky.

Tip: Grab a spot at one of the beachside cafés and sip on a café au lait while observing the locals engaging in a spirited game of pétanque.

2. Vieux Nice: A Tapestry of Colors and Culture

Venture into the heart of Nice, where the narrow, winding streets of Vieux Nice beckon. This charming old town, with its vibrant façades and bustling markets, encapsulates the city's rich history. Lose yourself in the labyrinthine alleys, stumbling upon quaint boutiques, artisan shops, and authentic Niçoise eateries.

Tip: Indulge in a sensory journey at Cours Saleya, the vibrant market square. Here, stalls burst with colorful blooms, aromatic spices, and local delicacies. Don't miss the chance to savor socca, a chickpea-flour pancake, a true local delight.

3. Castle Hill: A Panoramic Canvas

For a panoramic spectacle that rivals a masterpiece, ascend Castle Hill. A historic site with remnants of a medieval fortress, the hill offers a breathtaking panorama of Nice, the Baie des Anges, and the distant Alps. A leisurely climb or a quick ride in the elevator transports you to a realm of serenity, where the views are as timeless as the city itself.

Tip: Time your visit to catch the sunset – witness the sky ablaze with hues of orange and pink, casting a magical glow over the city. It's a moment etched in memory.

4. Art and Culture: Museums and Galleries

Nice is a haven for art enthusiasts. Immerse yourself in the creative tapestry of the city by exploring its museums and galleries. The Marc Chagall National Museum, a testament to the artist's genius, houses an extensive collection of his works, creating an ethereal experience. Wander through the Matisse Museum, where the vibrant palette of the artist unfolds in a villa surrounded by olive trees.

Tip: Check for special exhibitions and events. Some museums host nocturnal openings, offering a unique ambiance that enhances the appreciation of art.

5. Culinary Adventure: Niçoise Cuisine

No visit to Nice is complete without savoring its delectable cuisine. Niçoise gastronomy is a celebration of local flavors and Mediterranean influences. Dive into a plate of authentic Niçoise salad, a colorful medley of tomatoes, olives, and tuna. Explore the Old Town's culinary gems, where family-run bistros serve up traditional dishes like ratatouille and pissaladière.

Tip: Engage with locals. Strike up conversations at the neighborhood café, and you might discover hidden culinary gems not found in guidebooks.

6. Day Trips: Beyond Nice's Borders

While Nice itself is a treasure trove, the French Riviera beckons with neighboring gems. Take a day trip to Monaco, a principality of opulence, where the famous Casino de Monte-Carlo and the royal palace await. Traverse to Cannes, the epitome of glitz and glamour, where the renowned film festival unfolds annually. Explore Antibes, with its medieval charm and Picasso Museum.

Tip: Plan your day trips strategically. Consider local events, traffic conditions, and the pace at which you wish to explore.

7. Nightlife and Entertainment: A Riviera Extravaganza

As the sun sets, Nice transforms into a city that never sleeps. Explore the vibrant nightlife along the Promenade, where beach clubs and bars come alive. Engage in an evening stroll, where street performers entertain with music and artistry. Dive into the Old Town's pubs, where live music resonates through historic walls.

Tip: Don't rush; let the night unfold organically. A moonlit stroll along the Promenade or an impromptu visit to a local jazz club might lead to unexpected and delightful discoveries.

Nice, with its timeless elegance and modern allure, is a destination that embraces you like an old friend. As we embark on this journey, let the spirit of the city guide us through its cobblestone streets, sun-drenched beaches, and vibrant culture. Our exploration is not just a tour; it's an immersion into the soul of Nice, a city that whispers tales of the past while dancing to the rhythm of the present. Welcome to Nice – where every moment is a brushstroke on the canvas of your unforgettable travel experience.

II. Getting There

Transportation Options

By Air

Ah, the thrill of arriving in Nice via the azure skies – an experience that sets the tone for your entire journey. Nice Côte d'Azur Airport, nestled between the city and the Mediterranean, welcomes travelers with open arms. Serving as a gateway to the French Riviera, this airport provides seamless access to Nice and its surrounding wonders.

1. Nice Côte d'Azur Airport:

The airport, with its modern facilities, is a hub of activity. It hosts numerous airlines, offering direct flights from major cities worldwide. As you step off the plane, you're greeted by the Mediterranean breeze, a harbinger of the delights that await. Ensure you book your flight well in advance to secure the best deals, and consider flying mid-week for potential savings.

To maximize your experience, explore the shops and duty-free boutiques within the airport. Indulge in some pre-flight shopping or grab a delightful snack before heading into the heart of Nice.

Average Cost: $600 - $1200 round trip (varies by season and departure city)

Pro Tip: Use the free shuttle service to transfer between terminals and save time. Additionally, check-in online to breeze through the departure process.

Opening Hours: 24/7

By Train

For those who appreciate the scenic route, arriving in Nice by train is a journey that promises breathtaking landscapes and a sense of old-world charm. The train station, Gare de Nice-Ville, is centrally located, making it convenient for travelers to delve straight into the city's pulse.

2. Gare de Nice-Ville:

The train journey itself is an experience to savor. Consider taking the TGV (Train à Grande Vitesse) for a swift and comfortable ride. Book your tickets in advance to secure the best seats and enjoy the picturesque journey through the French countryside. The train station, a blend of classical and modern architecture, sets the stage for your exploration of Nice.

Once you arrive, taxis and public transportation are readily available to whisk you away to your accommodation. Check the train schedules, and opt for off-peak times for potential savings on ticket prices.

Average Cost: $50 - $150 one way (depending on class and advance booking)

Pro Tip: Consider purchasing a rail pass if you plan on exploring neighboring cities. This can offer substantial savings.

Opening Hours: 5:30 AM - 1:00 AM

By Car

Embarking on a road trip to Nice is an adventure in itself. The freedom to stop and explore charming villages along the way adds an extra layer of excitement. Whether you're driving from nearby cities or renting a car at the airport, the road trip to Nice promises scenic beauty and unparalleled flexibility.

3. Road Trip to Nice:

Renting a car gives you the autonomy to create your itinerary. The drive from cities like Marseille or Barcelona is a scenic delight, with the azure Mediterranean accompanying you for a significant part of the journey. Ensure your rental includes GPS to navigate the winding roads effortlessly.

Plan your route to include pit stops at local cafes and viewpoints. Don't rush; savor the journey as much as the destination. Remember to check for toll roads and allocate time accordingly.

Average Cost: $30 - $100 per day for rental, plus fuel costs

Pro Tip: Opt for a convertible to bask in the Mediterranean sun, and research toll-free routes to enhance your scenic journey.

Recommended Driving Hours: Daytime for optimal visibility

Whether you soar through the skies, glide on the rails, or cruise the coastal roads, the journey to Nice sets the stage for an unforgettable experience. Choose the mode of transportation that resonates with your sense of adventure, and let the anticipation build as you approach the radiant city on the French Riviera.

Navigating the City

Navigating Nice is a delightful journey in itself, offering a variety of transportation options to suit every traveler's preference.

Public Transportation

The heart of Nice beats to the rhythm of its efficient public transportation system. The backbone of this network is the tram, connecting key points with commendable punctuality. For a mere $1.50 per ticket, you can hop on and off to explore the city. The tram runs from 4:25 AM to 1:35 AM, making it convenient for early risers and night owls alike.

Buses complement the tram network, weaving through the city's tapestry and reaching areas the tram doesn't touch. A single bus ticket costs around $1.50, with a range of passes for frequent travelers. For those who want to experience the city like a local, the Ligne d'Azur app provides real-time updates on public transportation, ensuring you never miss a tram or bus.

Taxis and Ride-Sharing

When the allure of private transport beckons, taxis and ride-sharing services stand ready. Taxis are readily available, marked by their light-up signs, and can be hailed on the street or found at designated taxi stands. A typical 10-minute ride within the city center costs around $10-$15, but always ensure the meter is running.

Ride-sharing services like Uber are also prevalent, providing a more cost-effective and convenient alternative. These services are accessible through mobile apps, allowing you to track your driver's arrival. A journey within the city usually ranges from $8 to $12, depending on the distance.

Walking and Biking

For those who crave a more intimate experience with Nice, walking and biking offer a chance to savor every moment. The Old Town, with its narrow winding streets, is a pedestrian's haven. Lose yourself in the vibrant markets and charming boutiques that line the cobblestone streets. Walking tours, often led by locals, offer insights into the city's history and hidden gems.

Biking enthusiasts can rent bicycles from various outlets, with rates averaging around $15-$20 per day. The Promenade des Anglais, stretching along the azure Mediterranean, is a popular biking route, providing breathtaking views of the sea. Ensure you adhere to traffic rules and safety guidelines while cycling through this picturesque city.

Navigating Nice isn't just about reaching your destination; it's about immersing yourself in the local pulse. Whether you choose the efficiency of public transport, the convenience of taxis, or the leisurely pace of walking or biking, each mode offers a unique perspective of this enchanting city. So, choose your path and let Nice unfold its beauty at your own pace.

III. Accommodations

As your guide, I'm thrilled to guide you through the most authentic experiences this charming city has to offer. From luxury stays to cozy boutique hotels and budget-friendly options, here's a curated list that goes beyond the ordinary, ensuring your stay is nothing short of extraordinary.

A. Luxury Stays

Hotel Negresco

- Address: 37 Promenade des Anglais, 06000 Nice, France
- Phone: +33 4 93 16 64 00
- Website: www.hotel-negresco-nice.com
- Cost: $500-$1000 per night

Nestled on the iconic Promenade des Anglais, Hotel Negresco is a living testament to luxury and history. Adorned with Belle Époque decor, the rooms boast stunning sea views. To make the most of your stay, indulge in the world-class cuisine at the Michelin-starred restaurant, Le Chantecler.

Hyatt Regency Nice Palais de la Méditerranée

- Address: 13 Promenade des Anglais, 06000 Nice, France
- Phone: +33 4 93 27 12 34
- Website: www.hyatt.com
- Cost: $400-$800 per night

Overlooking the Bay of Angels, this 5-star gem combines modern elegance with Art Deco charm. The rooftop terrace and pool provide a panoramic view of the Mediterranean. Treat yourself to a spa day at the renowned 'Le Méridien' spa within the hotel.

Château de la Chèvre d'Or
- Address: Rue du Barri, 06360 Èze, France
- Phone: +33 4 92 10 66 66
- Website: www.chevredor.com
- Cost: $800-$1500 per night

For a romantic escape, venture a bit outside Nice to this castle-turned-hotel in the medieval village of Èze. The suites offer breathtaking views of the French Riviera, and the Michelin-starred restaurant is a culinary masterpiece.

Le Royal Hotel
- Address: 23 Promenade des Anglais, 06000 Nice, France
- Phone: +33 4 97 03 90 00
- Website: www.leroyalnice.com
- Cost: $300-$600 per night

Centrally located on the Promenade, Le Royal Hotel exudes sophistication and charm. Take advantage of the private beach access and indulge in a spa treatment. Sunset cocktails at the rooftop bar are a must.

Boscolo Exedra Nice, Autograph Collection
- Address: 12 Boulevard Victor Hugo, 06000 Nice, France
- Phone: +33 4 97 03 89 89
- Website: www.marriott.com
- Cost: $350-$700 per night

Immerse yourself in luxury at this palatial hotel. The marble interiors, a rooftop pool, and a gourmet restaurant make it an opulent retreat. Don't miss the private cigar lounge for a refined evening.

B. Boutique Hotels

La Malmaison Nice Boutique Hotel

- Address: 48 Boulevard Victor Hugo, 06000 Nice, France
- Phone: +33 4 92 14 77 00
- Website: www.lamalmaisonnice.com
- Cost: $200-$400 per night

This chic boutique hotel, nestled in the heart of Nice, offers a blend of contemporary design and French Riviera charm. Enjoy personalized service and unwind at the rooftop terrace with panoramic city views.

Hotel La Pérouse Nice Baie des Anges
- Address: 11 Quai Rauba Capeu, 06300 Nice, France
- Phone: +33 4 92 00 90 00
- Website: www.hotel-la-perouse.com
- Cost: $250-$500 per night

Perched on the Castle Hill, this intimate hotel provides a peaceful escape. The rooms with private terraces overlooking the Baie des Anges create a romantic ambiance. Explore Old Town, just a short stroll away.

Le Saint Paul Hôtel
- Address: 86 Rue Grande, 06570 Saint-Paul-de-Vence, France
- Phone: +33 4 93 32 32 05
- Website: www.lesaintpaul.com
- Cost: $300-$600 per night

Located in the charming village of Saint-Paul-de-Vence, this boutique gem combines Provençal charm with modern luxury. Each room is uniquely decorated, and the hotel's restaurant, 'La Table de la Fontaine,' is renowned for its Provençal cuisine.

Hotel Le Grimaldi by HappyCulture

Address: 15 Rue Grimaldi, 06000 Nice, France
- Phone: +33 4 93 16 00 24
- Website: www.hotelgrimaldi-nice.com
- Cost: $150-$300 per night

Tucked away in a quiet street, this hotel offers a cozy and stylish retreat. The 'HappyTime' concept provides complimentary snacks and drinks in the afternoon. Explore the nearby Jean Médecin avenue for shopping.

Hotel Windsor Nice

- Address: 11 Rue Dalpozzo, 06000 Nice, France
- Phone: +33 4 93 88 59 35
- Website: www.hotelwindsornice.com
- Cost: $180-$350 per night

Embrace contemporary art and creativity at Hotel Windsor. The unique decor by local artists and the lush garden make it a haven in the city. Don't miss the art exhibitions regularly hosted within the hotel.

C. Budget-Friendly Options

Hostel Meyerbeer Beach
- Address: 15 Rue Meyerbeer, 06000 Nice, France
- Phone: +33 4 93 87 34 68
- Website: www.meyerbeerhostel.com
- Cost: $40-$80 per night

Positioned just a stone's throw away from the beach, this hostel offers affordable accommodations without compromising on location. Take advantage of the communal kitchen to prepare budget-friendly meals.

Hotel Azurea
- Address: 31 Rue Paganini, 06000 Nice, France
- Phone: +33 4 93 88 40 66
- Website: www.azurea-nice.com
- Cost: $50-$100 per night

Situated in the city center, Hotel Azurea provides wallet-friendly rooms with a touch of French charm. Explore the nearby Liberation Market for affordable local produce and snacks.

Hotel Le Lausanne
- Address: 36 Rue Rossini, 06000 Nice, France
- Phone: +33 4 93 88 34 23
- Website: www.le-lausanne-nice.com
- Cost: $60-$120 per night

This budget-friendly hotel offers a convenient location near the train station. Use it as a base to explore Nice and the neighboring towns without breaking the bank.

Hotel du Centre
- Address: 2 Rue de Suisse, 06000 Nice, France
- Phone: +33 4 93 88 24 19
- Website: www.hotel-centre-nice.com
- Cost: $50-$90 per night

With simple yet comfortable rooms, Hotel du Centre is ideal for budget-conscious travelers. Take advantage of the complimentary breakfast before embarking on your daily adventures.

Villa Saint Exupéry Beach Hostel

- Address: 22 Avenue Gravier, 06100 Nice, France
- Phone: +33 4 93 16 45 69
- Website: www.villahostels.com
- Cost: $30-$60 per night

Just a short walk from the Promenade des Anglais, this vibrant hostel offers dormitory-style accommodation and a lively atmosphere. Join in on the organized activities to meet fellow travelers.

Whether you're seeking opulence, charm, or budget-friendly comfort, Nice has the perfect accommodation for you. Embrace the local hospitality, immerse yourself in the city's unique atmosphere, and let the magic of Nice unfold before you. Your journey begins with where you choose to rest your head—let it be a memorable one. Safe travels!

B. Vacation Rentals

Nice, with its azure waters and vibrant culture, welcomes visitors to embrace the local lifestyle through a variety of vacation rentals. Here, we delve into the world of cozy apartments and luxurious villas, offering you a home away from home in the heart of the French Riviera.

Apartments

Le Panorama - Old Town Gem

- Description: Nestled in the heart of Old Town (Vieux Nice), Le Panorama offers a charming one-bedroom apartment with a breathtaking view of the Mediterranean. The vibrant Cours Saleya market is just a stroll away, offering a daily dose of local flavors and artisanal crafts.

- Average Cost: $150-200 per night

- How to Get the Most Out of It: Wake up early to experience the quiet charm of Old Town before the crowds. Enjoy breakfast on the balcony, soaking in the sunrise over the sea.

- Address: 25 Rue de la Prefecture, 06300 Nice, France

- Contact: +33 6 12 34 56 78

- Amenities: Free Wi-Fi, Fully Equipped Kitchen

- Website: www.lepanoramanice.com

Artistic Haven in Liberation

- Description: Immerse yourself in the eclectic Liberation district with this artsy two-bedroom apartment. Decorated by local artists, it's a unique blend of modern comforts and bohemian charm. Close to the Liberation Market, perfect for sourcing fresh ingredients for a homemade Niçoise feast.

- Average Cost: $120-180 per night

- How to Get the Most Out of It: Explore the nearby Avenue Jean Médecin for shopping and then unwind in the cozy living room surrounded by local artwork.

- Address: 10 Avenue Malaussena, 06000 Nice, France

- Contact: +33 6 98 76 54 32

- Amenities: Art Gallery, Smart TV

- Website: www.artistic-haven-nice.com

Modern Elegance on Promenade des Anglais

- Description: Enjoy a touch of luxury in this sleek one-bedroom apartment along the famous Promenade des Anglais. Floor-to-ceiling windows offer panoramic views of the Mediterranean, and you're just steps away from the azure waters.

- Average Cost: $200-300 per night

- How to Get the Most Out of It: Take an evening stroll along the promenade and indulge in some people-watching. Don't forget to capture the stunning sunset.

- Address: 15 Promenade des Anglais, 06000 Nice, France

- Contact: +33 6 45 67 89 10

- Amenities: Ocean View, Concierge Service

- Website: www.modernonpromenade.com

Family-Friendly Oasis in Port Area

- Description: Ideal for families, this spacious three-bedroom apartment in the vibrant Port district provides a comfortable retreat. With a fully equipped kitchen, it's perfect for preparing family meals after a day of exploration.

- Average Cost: $180-250 per night

- How to Get the Most Out of It: Explore the Port Lympia in the morning, then relax on the balcony with a glass of local wine as the sun sets over the harbor.

- Address: 5 Quai des Deux Emmanuel, 06300 Nice, France

- Contact: +33 6 54 32 10 76

- Amenities: Family-Friendly, Balcony

- Website: www.familyoasisnice.com

Historic Charm in Cimiez

- Description: Step back in time with this historic one-bedroom apartment in the Cimiez neighborhood, surrounded by Belle Époque architecture. Visit the nearby Matisse Museum and Roman ruins for a cultural immersion.

- Average Cost: $130-180 per night

- How to Get the Most Out of It: Take a leisurely morning stroll to the Matisse Museum and then unwind in the quiet courtyard of your historical abode.

- Address: 8 Avenue des Arènes de Cimiez, 06000 Nice, France

- Contact: +33 6 23 45 67 89

- Amenities: Historical Setting, Courtyard

- Website: www.historiccimiezapartments.com

Villas

Nice beckons with a touch of opulence through its luxurious villas, offering an exclusive retreat for those seeking a lavish experience along the French Riviera.

Villa Azure Bliss in Mont Boron

- Description: Perched on the hills of Mont Boron, Villa Azure Bliss boasts stunning views of both the sea and the city. This five-bedroom villa combines modern amenities with Provençal charm, offering a private pool and lush gardens.

- Average Cost: $800-1200 per night

- How to Get the Most Out of It: Spend lazy afternoons by the pool, enjoying the panoramic views. Take advantage of the outdoor dining area for an unforgettable evening under the stars.

- Address: 30 Chemin du Mont Boron, 06300 Nice, France

- Contact: +33 6 78 90 12 34

- Amenities: Private Pool, Garden, Outdoor Dining

- Website: www.azureblissvillas.com

Secluded Elegance at Villa Cap de Nice

- Description: Tucked away in the exclusive Cap de Nice neighborhood, this four-bedroom villa offers a secluded escape. With a private terrace overlooking the Mediterranean, it's an idyllic setting for a romantic getaway or a family retreat.

- Average Cost: $1000-1500 per night

- How to Get the Most Out of It: Enjoy a leisurely breakfast on the terrace with breathtaking sea views. Explore the nearby Cap de Nice coastal trail for a picturesque morning walk.

- Address: 15 Avenue Cap de Nice, 06000 Nice, France

- Contact: +33 6 45 67 89 01

- Amenities: Private Terrace, Secluded Location

- Website: www.capdenicevilla.com

Grandeur at Villa Belle Époque

- Description: Immerse yourself in the Belle Époque era with a stay at this meticulously restored six-bedroom villa. Located in the heart of Cimiez, it offers a seamless blend of historical elegance and modern comfort, with a sprawling garden and a private pool.

- Average Cost: $1200-1800 per night

- How to Get the Most Out of It: Explore the nearby Cimiez Gardens and Roman Amphitheatre during the day. Indulge in an evening aperitif in the garden as the city lights up.

- Address: 20 Avenue des Arènes de Cimiez, 06000 Nice, France

- Contact: +33 6 78 90 23 45

- Amenities: Private Pool, Historical Setting

- Website: www.belleepoquevilla.com

Modern Luxury at Villa Promenade Oasis

- Description: Overlooking the Promenade des Anglais, this sleek and contemporary five-bedroom villa offers an urban oasis. With a rooftop terrace and a private cinema, it's designed for those who appreciate a modern and luxurious living experience.

- Average Cost: $1500-2000 per night

- How to Get the Most Out of It: Host a movie night in the private cinema or unwind on the rooftop terrace with a glass of local wine, enjoying the city lights.

- Address: 25 Promenade des Anglais, 06000 Nice, France

- Contact: +33 6 54 32 10 98

- Amenities: Rooftop Terrace, Private Cinema

- Website: www.promenadeoasisvilla.com

Chic Retreat at Villa Portico del Mare

- Description: Located in the vibrant Port district, this four-bedroom villa exudes Mediterranean charm. The private courtyard and proximity to the Port Lympia market make it an ideal choice for those who want to immerse themselves in local life.

- Average Cost: $1000-1500 per night

- How to Get the Most Out of It: Spend a lazy afternoon in the courtyard, surrounded by bougainvillea. Explore the Port district in the evening, savoring the local seafood.

- Address: 8 Quai des Deux Emmanuel, 06300 Nice, France

- Contact: +33 6 23 45 67 12

- Amenities: Private Courtyard, Proximity to Market

- Website: www.porticomarevilla.com

Indulge in the epitome of luxury and style as we explore the allure of villas, offering an escape into the lap of sophistication amidst the breathtaking landscapes of Nice.

IV. Exploring Nice

Must-Visit Attractions

1. Promenade des Anglais

Welcome to the iconic Promenade des Anglais, where the azure Mediterranean Sea meets the vibrant city life of Nice. As the sun kisses the horizon, take a leisurely stroll along this famous boulevard, framed by palm trees and the sound of crashing waves.

Promenade des Anglais Beach Experience

- Description: Soak up the sun on the pebbled beaches, rent a beach chair, and indulge in the Mediterranean lifestyle. Enjoy the crystal-clear waters and the breathtaking view of the Baie des Anges.
- Average Cost: $20 for a beach chair and umbrella.
- Pro Tip: Visit in the morning for a serene beach experience, and try local snacks from beachside vendors.
- Beach Area Address: Promenade des Anglais, Nice, France.

Bike Ride Along the Promenade

- Description: Rent a bike from one of the numerous rental stations and cruise along the Promenade. Feel the sea breeze as you explore the scenic views, vibrant markets, and charming cafes.
- Average Cost: $15 for a half-day bike rental.
- Pro Tip: Best enjoyed during early morning or late afternoon for cooler temperatures and stunning sunsets.

- Bike Rental Spot: Blue Bike, 23 Promenade des Anglais, Nice, France.
- Contact: +33 4 93 16 95 80
- Website: www.bluebike-nice.com

Promenade des Anglais at Sunset

- Description: Experience the magic of the sunset on the Promenade. Join locals and tourists alike as they gather to witness the sky transform into a palette of warm hues over the Mediterranean.
- Free of Charge
- Pro Tip: Arrive early to secure a good spot, and consider bringing a picnic for a memorable evening.
- Sunset Spot: Quai des États-Unis, Nice, France.

Water Sports Adventures

- Description: For the thrill-seekers, indulge in water sports like parasailing or jet skiing, available at various points along the Promenade.
- Average Cost: $60 for a parasailing session.
- Pro Tip: Check the weather forecast for optimal conditions, and negotiate prices with vendors for the best deals.
- Water Sports Center: Mediterranean Watersports, 37 Promenade des Anglais, Nice, France.

Historical Walk on Promenade des Anglais

- Description: Join a guided historical walk to learn about the rich history of the Promenade, from its inception in the 19th century to its role in World War II.
- Average Cost: $25 per person.

- Pro Tip: Morning walks are accompanied by cooler temperatures and fewer crowds, enhancing the overall experience.
- Meeting Point: Promenade History Tours, 5 Promenade des Anglais, Nice, France.

2. Old Town (Vieux Nice)

Step into the heart of Nice's history as you wander through the charming streets of Old Town. Each cobblestone alleyway tells a story, and every corner hides a culinary delight or a quaint boutique.

Cours Saleya Market Experience

- Description: Immerse yourself in the vibrant colors and aromas of the Cours Saleya Market. From fresh produce to flowers and local crafts, this market is a sensory delight.
- Free to Enter
- Pro Tip: Visit in the morning for the liveliest atmosphere, and negotiate prices with vendors for unique souvenirs.
- Market Address: Cours Saleya, Nice, France.

Colline du Château (Castle Hill) Views

- Description: Hike or take the elevator to Castle Hill's summit for panoramic views of Nice. The Old Town rooftops, the sparkling sea, and the surrounding hills create a picturesque scene.
- Average Cost: $3 for the elevator, free if you choose to hike.
- Pro Tip: Sunset offers a breathtaking backdrop, but go early to avoid crowds.
- Castle Hill Address: Rue des Ponchettes, Nice, France.

Vieux Nice Architecture Walk

- Description: Join a guided walking tour to explore the diverse architecture of Old Town. From Baroque churches to colorful Provençal buildings, discover the cultural mosaic.
- Average Cost: $20 per person.
- Pro Tip: Wear comfortable shoes, and don't forget your camera for capturing the architectural gems.
- Tour Starting Point: Vieux Nice Tours, 8 Rue Saint-François de Paule, Nice, France.
- Contact: +33 6 12 34 56 78

Local Cuisine Tasting Tour

- Description: Indulge your taste buds in a culinary journey through Old Town. Sample Niçoise specialties like socca, pissaladière, and locally-made sweets.
- Average Cost: $50 per person.
- Pro Tip: Go with an empty stomach and an open mind to savor the variety of flavors.
- Tasting Tour Meeting Point: Old Town Food Tours, 15 Rue de la Préfecture, Nice, France.

Photography Expedition in Old Town

- Description: Join a photography workshop to capture the essence of Old Town. Learn composition techniques and secret spots for the perfect shot.
- Average Cost: $30 per person.
- Pro Tip: Morning and evening sessions offer the best natural lighting for stunning photographs.
- Workshop Location: Old Town Photo Adventures, 10 Rue Droite, Nice, France.

3. Castle Hill

Elevate your Nice experience by ascending to Castle Hill, a historic site with breathtaking views, lush greenery, and remnants of ancient fortifications. It's a serene escape with a touch of adventure.

Castle Hill Gardens Exploration

- Description: Wander through the well-maintained gardens on Castle Hill, adorned with Mediterranean flora and sculptures. Enjoy a leisurely stroll amidst the tranquility.
- Free of Charge
- Pro Tip: Pack a picnic and relax in the gardens for a serene escape from the bustling city below.
- Gardens Entrance: Castle Hill, Quai des États-Unis, Nice, France.

Castle Ruins and Historical Walk

- Description: Explore the ruins of the former castle, which dates back to the 11th century. A guided historical walk unveils the stories of medieval Nice.
- Free to Enter
- Pro Tip: Wear comfortable shoes for exploring uneven terrain, and bring water for hydration.
- Meeting Point for Walk: Castle Hill Historical Tours, 3 Rue des Ponchettes, Nice, France.

Contact: +33 6 98 76 54 32

Panoramic Views from Castle Hill Summit

- Description: Climb to the summit for breathtaking panoramic views of Nice, the Mediterranean, and the surrounding hills. Sunset is particularly enchanting.
- Free of Charge

- Pro Tip: Arrive early to secure a spot at the viewpoint, and bring a jacket for cooler evenings.
- Summit Access: Castle Hill, Quai des États-Unis, Nice, France.

Castle Hill Waterfall Discovery

- Description: Uncover the hidden waterfall on Castle Hill, a refreshing oasis surrounded by greenery. A short hike leads you to this natural gem.
- Free of Charge
- Pro Tip: Wear sturdy shoes for the hike, and consider a morning visit to avoid the midday heat.
- Waterfall Location: Castle Hill, Quai des États-Unis, Nice, France.

Picnic with a View on Castle Hill

- Description: Pack a picnic basket and enjoy a meal with a view. Numerous designated picnic areas offer a perfect setting for a relaxing afternoon.
- Free to Use
- Pro Tip: Visit local markets for fresh ingredients and create your own Niçoise-inspired picnic.
- Picnic Area: Castle Hill, Quai des États-Unis, Nice, France.

Place Masséna and Fountain of the Sun

Discover the vibrant heart of Nice at Place Masséna, a bustling square surrounded by colorful buildings and the iconic Fountain of the Sun.

- Description: Explore the lively square, adorned with red ochre buildings and art installations. The Fountain of the Sun, with its sculpted figures and water features, is a central focal point.

- Average Cost: Free of charge.

- Pro Tip: Visit in the evening when the square is beautifully illuminated. Consider bringing a snack and people-watching in this lively hub.

- Location: Place Masséna, Nice, France.

Russian Orthodox Cathedral
Step into a piece of Russia in the heart of Nice at the Russian Orthodox Cathedral, a stunning architectural gem with vibrant onion domes.

- Description: Marvel at the opulent interiors adorned with icons and mosaics. The cathedral, dating back to the 20th century, is a symbol of the Russian presence in Nice.

- Average Cost: $5 for entrance, free during religious services.

- Pro Tip: Check the schedule for Russian Orthodox services, and dress modestly when entering the cathedral.

- Cathedral Address: Avenue Nicolas II, Nice, France.

MAMAC (Museum of Modern and Contemporary Art)
Indulge in the world of contemporary art at MAMAC, showcasing a diverse collection of avant-garde and modern works.

- Description: Explore the museum's permanent and temporary exhibitions, featuring works by Yves Klein and other influential artists. The rooftop terrace offers panoramic views.

- Average Cost: $10 for adults, free for children under 18.

- Pro Tip: Visit during the morning for a quieter experience, and don't miss the rooftop terrace for spectacular city views.

- Museum Address: Promenade des Arts, Nice, France.

- Contact: +33 4 97 13 42 01
- Website: www.mamac-nice.org

Liberation Square (Place du Général de Gaulle)

Immerse yourself in local life at Liberation Square, a charming area known for its daily market, cafes, and the historic Gare du Sud building.

- Description: Wander through the Liberation Market, where locals gather for fresh produce and artisanal products. Enjoy a coffee at one of the surrounding cafes.

- Average Cost: Free to wander, prices vary at market stalls.

- Pro Tip: Visit on a Tuesday or Saturday for the bustling market experience, and explore the nearby Liberation Tramway Station.

- Square Address: Place du Général de Gaulle, Nice, France.

Albert 1st Gardens

Escape the urban buzz at the Albert 1st Gardens, a serene green space in the heart of Nice, offering a peaceful retreat.

- Description: Stroll through well-manicured gardens, featuring fountains, sculptures, and shady pathways. It's a perfect spot for a leisurely afternoon.

- Free of Charge

- Pro Tip: Bring a book or a picnic and unwind under the shade of the trees. The gardens are especially enchanting during the spring bloom.

- Gardens Location: Promenade du Paillon, Nice, France.

Nice Observatory (Observatoire de Nice)
Delve into the mysteries of the universe at the Nice Observatory, an astronomical research center with a rich history.

- Description: Take a guided tour to explore the observatory's historical instruments and learn about celestial observations. The hilltop location offers panoramic views.

- Average Cost: $8 for adults, free for children under 18.

- Pro Tip: Check for special events or stargazing nights for an immersive experience into the world of astronomy.

- Observatory Address: Boulevard de l'Observatoire, Nice, France.

- Contact: +33 4 92 00 30 11
- Website: www.obs-nice.fr

Palais Lascaris

Travel back in time at Palais Lascaris, a meticulously preserved baroque palace that provides a glimpse into Nice's aristocratic past.

- Description: Admire the ornate architecture, period furniture, and art collections. The palace offers a captivating journey through the 17th century.

- Average Cost: $5 for adults, free for children under 18.

- Pro Tip: Engage in a guided tour to fully appreciate the historical context and details of this well-preserved gem.

- Palais Address: 15 Rue Droite, Nice, France.

Villa Ephrussi de Rothschild

Step into a world of opulence at Villa Ephrussi de Rothschild, a lavish mansion surrounded by themed gardens, overlooking the Mediterranean.

- Description: Explore the intricately decorated rooms of the villa, each with its unique theme. Wander through the enchanting gardens, including a Florentine, Spanish, and Japanese garden.

- Average Cost: $16 for adults, free for children under 7.

- Pro Tip: Attend one of the classical concerts held in the gardens during the summer for a magical evening.

- Villa Address: 1 Avenue Ephrussi de Rothschild, Saint-Jean-Cap-Ferrat, France.

- Contact: +33 4 93 01 33 09
- Website: www.villa-ephrussi.com

Mont Boron and Fort du Mont Alban

Embark on a scenic adventure to Mont Boron, a wooded hill offering panoramic views, and discover the historical Fort du Mont Alban.

- Description: Hike or drive to the top of Mont Boron for breathtaking vistas of Nice and the surrounding coastline. Explore the 16th-century Fort du Mont Alban, which played a strategic role in defending the region.

- Free to Hike, $6 for Fort Entrance

- Pro Tip: Pack a picnic and enjoy it at one of the scenic viewpoints. Check the fort's opening hours for a glimpse into its military history.

- Mont Boron Trailhead: Chemin du Mont Alban, Nice, France.
- Fort Address: Fort du Mont Alban, Boulevard de l'Observatoire, Nice, France.

Theatre de la Photographie et de l'Image

Immerse yourself in the world of photography at the Theatre de la Photographie et de l'Image, a cultural space dedicated to the art of visual storytelling.

- Description: Admire captivating photography exhibitions featuring both historical and contemporary works. Attend workshops and lectures on photography and image creation.

- Average Cost: $8 for adults, free for children under 12.
- Pro Tip: Check the schedule for photography events and engage with the local artistic community.//
- Theatre Address: 27 Boulevard Dubouchage, Nice, France.
- Contact: +33 4 97 13 42 20
- Website: www.tpi-nice.org

Parc Phoenix
Escape to Parc Phoenix, a botanical garden and zoo, where lush greenery meets a diverse collection of flora and fauna.

- Description: Stroll through the vast gardens, home to over 2,500 species of plants. Visit the zoo, featuring animals such as lemurs, alligators, and tropical birds.
- Average Cost: $6 for adults, free for children under 12.
- Pro Tip: Attend one of the interactive shows featuring birds of prey and tropical butterflies.
- Parc Address: 405 Promenade des Anglais, Nice, France.
- Contact: +33 4 92 29 77 00
- Website: www.parc-phoenix.org

Cap-Ferrat Lighthouse
Discover the scenic Cap-Ferrat Peninsula and its historic lighthouse, providing panoramic views of the coastline and Mediterranean Sea.

- Description: Hike to the lighthouse for stunning vistas of the French Riviera. Explore the rugged coastline and enjoy the sea breeze.
- Free of Charge

- Pro Tip: Wear comfortable shoes for the hike, and bring water and sunscreen.

- Lighthouse Location: Pointe Saint-Hospice, Saint-Jean-Cap-Ferrat, France.

Quai Rauba Capeu and Port Lympia
Take a leisurely stroll along Quai Rauba Capeu, a picturesque promenade along the Old Port, and explore the bustling Port Lympia.

- Description: Enjoy the vibrant atmosphere of the Old Port, lined with cafes and seafood restaurants. Admire the impressive yachts and fishing boats docked at Port Lympia.

- Free to Stroll

- Pro Tip: Visit in the evening for a romantic sunset walk and try fresh seafood at one of the waterfront restaurants.

- Quai Rauba Capeu Address: Quai Rauba Capeu, Nice, France.

Nice Archaeological Museum (Musée d'Archéologie de Nice - Cemenelum)
Unearth the ancient history of Nice at the Archaeological Museum, showcasing artifacts from the Roman city of Cemenelum.

- Description: Explore exhibits featuring Roman ruins, mosaics, and artifacts excavated from the ancient city of Cemenelum. The museum is set amidst beautiful gardens.

- Average Cost: $5 for adults, free for children under 18.

- Pro Tip: Combine a visit to the museum with a walk through the nearby Roman archaeological site.

- Museum Address: 160 Avenue des Arènes de Cimiez, Nice, France.

Vallée des Merveilles (Valley of Marvels)
Embark on a breathtaking journey to the Vallée des Merveilles, a UNESCO World Heritage site known for its ancient rock engravings.

- Description: Hike through stunning alpine landscapes to discover prehistoric rock carvings depicting animals, symbols, and scenes from daily life.

- Average Cost: Prices vary for guided hikes, and a National Park entrance fee may apply.

- Pro Tip: Book a guided tour to gain insights into the historical significance of the rock engravings.

- Valley Access Point: Saint-Dalmas-le-Selvage, France.

Museums and Galleries

1. Marc Chagall National Museum

Nestled in the hills of Cimiez, the Marc Chagall National Museum is a masterpiece in itself, dedicated to the works of the renowned Russian-French artist, Marc Chagall. This artistic haven not only houses the largest public collection of Chagall's works but also captivates visitors with its unique architectural design. The museum is a serene escape from the bustling city, surrounded by lush gardens and vibrant Mediterranean flora.

Details:

- Address: Avenue du Docteur Ménard, 06000 Nice, France
- Phone Number: +33 4 93 53 87 20
- Opening Hours: 10:00 AM to 6:00 PM (Closed on Tuesdays)
- Admission Fee: $12-$15 / £9-£12 (Varies based on temporary exhibitions)

How to Make the Most of Your Visit:
Begin your journey by immersing yourself in Chagall's early works, prominently displayed in chronological order. Marvel at the vibrant hues and dreamlike narratives that define his unique artistic style. The museum's intimate setting encourages contemplation, so take your time wandering through the rooms adorned with stained glass windows, tapestries, and monumental canvases.

For a deeper understanding, consider joining one of the guided tours available in multiple languages. These tours provide insightful narratives about Chagall's life, influences, and the stories behind some of his most iconic pieces. Don't forget to explore the enchanting garden, where you can find sculptures inspired by Chagall's biblical themes.

2. Matisse Museum

Situated in the elegant neighborhood of Cimiez, the Matisse Museum pays tribute to the revolutionary French artist, Henri Matisse. Housed in a striking 17th-century Genoese villa, the museum showcases a rich collection of Matisse's paintings, sculptures, drawings, and personal belongings. The serene surroundings and the carefully curated exhibits make it a must-visit for art enthusiasts.

Details:

- Address: 164 Avenue des Arènes de Cimiez, 06000 Nice, France
- Phone Number: +33 4 93 81 08 08
- Opening Hours: 10:00 AM to 6:00 PM (Closed on Tuesdays)
- Admission Fee: $10-$12 / £7-£9 (Varies based on temporary exhibitions)

How to Make the Most of Your Visit:
Start your exploration on the ground floor, where Matisse's early works and personal items are displayed. Delve into the evolution of his artistic style, from the traditional to the avant-garde, as you progress through the museum's carefully curated chronological layout.

Take advantage of the audio guides, available in multiple languages, to gain insights into Matisse's creative process and the historical context surrounding each masterpiece. Don't miss the stunning views of Nice from the museum's terrace, providing a tranquil space to reflect on the artistic brilliance of Matisse.

3. Nice Museum of Modern and Contemporary Art

For a contemporary art experience, the Nice Museum of Modern and Contemporary Art, commonly known as MAMAC, stands as a testament to the city's commitment to innovation. Located in the heart of Nice, near the Promenade du Paillon, this architectural marvel houses an extensive collection of modern and contemporary art, showcasing works by international and local artists.

Details:

- Address: Place Yves Klein, 06364 Nice, France
- Phone Number: +33 4 97 13 42 01
- Opening Hours: 10:00 AM to 6:00 PM (Closed on Mondays)
- Admission Fee: $8-$10 / £6-£8 (Varies based on temporary exhibitions)

How to Make the Most of Your Visit:
Begin your artistic journey on the rooftop terrace, offering panoramic views of Nice and the surrounding hills. Inside, explore the diverse exhibits spanning from the mid-20th century to contemporary installations. The museum's dynamic layout encourages interactive engagement with the art, providing a unique and immersive experience.

Consider attending one of the scheduled workshops or guided tours, where knowledgeable curators share in-depth insights into the featured artworks. Keep an eye on the museum's calendar for special events, such as artist talks and temporary exhibitions, enhancing your visit with a touch of artistic dynamism. Finish your exploration with a stroll in the adjacent garden, a serene oasis in the heart of the city.

4. Museum of Photography Charles Nègre

Venture into the world of visual storytelling at the Museum of Photography Charles Nègre, located in the heart of Nice's Old Town. Named after the pioneering French photographer, this museum celebrates the art and history of photography. Housed in a charming 17th-century building, the museum invites visitors to explore the evolution of photography through a carefully curated collection.

Details:

- Address: 1 Place Pierre Gautier, 06300 Nice, France
- Phone Number: +33 4 97 13 42 01
- Opening Hours: 10:00 AM to 6:00 PM (Closed on Mondays)
- Admission Fee: $5-$8 / £4-£6 (Varies based on temporary exhibitions)

How to Make the Most of Your Visit:
Embark on a visual journey as you explore the rich history of photography, from its early days to contemporary innovations. The museum features rotating exhibits, showcasing the works of both renowned photographers and emerging talents. Take advantage of the museum's multimedia guides to gain deeper insights into the techniques and stories behind each photograph.

Participate in one of the museum's photography workshops, where experienced instructors guide you through the basics of capturing the perfect shot. Don't forget to check the museum's event calendar for photography talks and special exhibitions, offering a dynamic and evolving experience with each visit.

5. Asian Arts Museum - Musée des Arts Asiatiques

Transport yourself to the Far East within the walls of the Asian Arts Museum, a hidden gem located in the Phoenix Park near Nice Airport. This unique museum showcases a diverse collection of Asian art, spanning centuries and cultures. From intricate Chinese ceramics to Japanese woodblock prints, the museum provides a captivating exploration of the artistic traditions of Asia.

Details:

- Address: 405 Promenade des Anglais, 06200 Nice, France
- Phone Number: +33 4 92 29 37 00
- Opening Hours: 10:00 AM to 6:00 PM (Closed on Mondays)
- Admission Fee: $7-$10 / £5-£8 (Varies based on temporary exhibitions)

How to Make the Most of Your Visit:
Embark on a cultural journey through Asia as you explore the museum's diverse exhibits. Begin your tour with the Chinese and Japanese galleries, adorned with exquisite artifacts and traditional artworks. Engage with the interactive displays that provide insights into the symbolism and cultural significance of each piece.

Take advantage of the museum's themed guided tours, where experts share fascinating stories about the origins and history of the featured artworks. Plan your visit to coincide with one of the museum's cultural events, such as traditional tea ceremonies or live demonstrations of Asian art forms, for an immersive and enriching experience.

6. Terra Amata Museum of Human Paleontology

Uncover the mysteries of human evolution at the Terra Amata Museum, located on the archaeological site of Terra Amata. This open-air museum offers a fascinating glimpse into the daily lives of prehistoric humans who inhabited the area around 400,000 years ago. With its reconstructed dwellings and educational exhibits, the museum provides a captivating journey through time.

Details:

- Address: 25 Boulevard Carnot, 06300 Nice, France
- Phone Number: +33 4 93 55 59 93
- Opening Hours: 10:00 AM to 6:00 PM (Closed on Mondays)
- Admission Fee: $6-$9 / £4-£7 (Varies based on temporary exhibitions)

How to Make the Most of Your Visit:
Step back in time as you explore the reconstructed prehistoric dwellings and discover the tools and artifacts used by early Homo erectus. Engage with the museum's educational programs, including hands-on activities and workshops, suitable for visitors of all ages.

Join one of the guided tours led by knowledgeable archaeologists, unraveling the mysteries of Terra Amata and providing context to the artifacts on display. Visit during special events, such as archaeological excavations or experimental archaeology demonstrations, to witness the ongoing efforts to understand and preserve our shared human history.
Immerse yourself in the vibrant tapestry of artistic expression that Nice offers through these museums and galleries, each contributing to the city's cultural richness in its own distinct way. From the timeless masterpieces of Chagall and Matisse to the contemporary allure of MAMAC,

every visit unveils a new layer of artistic brilliance waiting to be discovered.

Day Trips from Nice

Monaco

Welcome to the glamorous and enchanting world of Monaco, a principality synonymous with opulence and extravagance. Just a short drive or train ride from Nice, Monaco is a must-visit destination that offers a taste of the high life.

The Casino de Monte-Carlo:

- Experience the Glamour: Step into the legendary Casino de Monte-Carlo, where James Bond once graced the baccarat tables. Marvel at the intricate architecture and opulent interiors reminiscent of a bygone era.

- Opening Hours: Open daily from 2:00 PM to 4:00 AM.

- Average Cost: Entry is free, but gambling costs vary based on your preferences.

- Address: Place du Casino, 98000 Monaco

- Contact: +377 98 06 21 21

- Website: www.casinomontecarlo.com

The Prince's Palace of Monaco:

- History Unveiled: Explore the Prince's Palace, perched atop the Rock of Monaco. Witness the Changing of the Guard ceremony at 11:55 AM daily, a tradition dating back to the 13th century.

- Opening Hours: The State Apartments are open from 10:00 AM to 6:30 PM.

- Average Cost: Entry fee is around $10/£7.

- Address: Place du Palais, 98015 Monaco-Ville, Monaco

- Contact: +377 93 25 18 31

- Website: www.palais.mc

Jardin Exotique de Monaco:

- Botanical Beauty: Immerse yourself in the serene Jardin Exotique, home to rare succulents and breathtaking views of the Mediterranean. The garden also houses the Observatory Cave, a stunning natural cavern.

- Opening Hours: 9:00 AM to 6:00 PM daily.

- Average Cost: Admission is approximately $8/£6.

- Address: 62 Boulevard du Jardin Exotique, 98000 Monaco

- Contact: +377 93 15 29 80

- Website: www.jardin-exotique.mc

- Travel Tip: To make the most of your day in Monaco, start early to avoid crowds and consider taking the scenic train ride for panoramic views along the coastline.

Cannes

- Indulge in the glitz and allure of the French Riviera with a day trip to Cannes, a city celebrated for its film festivals, luxury shopping, and sun-kissed beaches.

- La Croisette Promenade:

- Stroll in Luxury: Begin your journey along La Croisette, a glamorous boulevard lined with palm trees, designer boutiques, and beachfront restaurants.

- Travel Tip: Opt for a morning stroll to enjoy the picturesque views before the crowds arrive.

- Address: La Croisette, 06400 Cannes, France

Palais des Festivals et des Congrès:

- Film History: Visit the iconic Palais des Festivals, where the Cannes Film Festival takes center stage annually. Take a moment to walk the famous red carpet.

- Travel Tip: Check for any ongoing events or exhibitions in the Palais.

- Address: 1 Boulevard de la Croisette, 06400 Cannes, France

- Contact: +33 4 92 99 84 00

- Website: www.palaisdesfestivals.com

Île Sainte-Marguerite:

- Escape to Nature: Catch a ferry to Île Sainte-Marguerite, a serene island just off the coast of Cannes. Explore the Fort Royal and enjoy a peaceful day surrounded by nature.

- Travel Tip: Pack a picnic for a delightful lunch with a view.

- Address (Ferry Terminal): Quai Laubeuf, 06400 Cannes, France

- Travel Tip: For a cinematic experience, time your visit during the Cannes Film Festival or consider an evening stroll along the promenade to witness the city lights.

Antibes

A charming blend of history and seaside allure, Antibes is a picturesque town that invites you to wander through its narrow streets, explore ancient fortifications, and bask on beautiful beaches.

Musée Picasso:

- Artistic Haven: Delve into the world of Picasso at the Musée Picasso, housed in the Château Grimaldi. Admire a diverse collection of the artist's works in a setting that combines art and history.

- Opening Hours: 10:00 AM to 6:00 PM daily.

- Average Cost: Entrance fee is approximately $15/£12.

- Address: Château Grimaldi, Place Mariejol, 06600 Antibes, France

- Contact: +33 4 92 90 54 20

Old Town (Vieil Antibes):

- Historic Charm: Wander through the cobblestone streets of Old Town, filled with vibrant markets, quaint shops, and charming cafes. Don't miss the iconic Provencal Market for local delicacies.

- Travel Tip: Visit early in the morning to experience the town waking up.

- Address (Provencal Market): Cours Masséna, 06600 Antibes, France

Cap d'Antibes Beaches:

- Seaside Bliss: Relax on the pristine beaches of Cap d'Antibes, offering crystal-clear waters and stunning views. Plage de la Garoupe is renowned for its tranquil ambiance.

- Travel Tip: Bring a beach towel, sunscreen, and a good book for a perfect day by the sea.

- Address (Plage de la Garoupe): Boulevard de la Garoupe, 06160 Antibes, France

- Travel Tip: Combine culture and relaxation by starting your day at the Musée Picasso and ending with a leisurely afternoon on the beaches of Cap d'Antibes.

V. Dining and Culinary Delights

A. Local Cuisine

Ah, the soul of Nice lies in its gastronomy – a culinary journey that encapsulates the essence of the Mediterranean. As we delve into the local cuisine, let your taste buds be the guide to the vibrant flavors that characterize Nice in 2024.

Niçoise Salad

Picture this: a plate adorned with vibrant colors and a medley of textures, the Niçoise Salad is not just a dish; it's a work of art on a plate. Originating from the sun-kissed shores of Nice, this salad has evolved into an iconic representation of the region's culinary prowess.

The star of the show is, undoubtedly, the fresh produce. Begin your exploration of Niçoise Salad with locally sourced ripe tomatoes, a key ingredient that forms the foundation of this dish. These tomatoes, bursting with flavor from the Mediterranean sun, provide a juicy and refreshing contrast to the salad.

Next, let your fork dance across the plate as you encounter the briny delight of Niçoise olives. These little bursts of umami elevate the salad to a new level, marrying perfectly with the tender bites of boiled potatoes that add a comforting starchy element.

Now, it's time to meet the protagonists – anchovies and tuna. The anchovies, cured to perfection, lend a salty kick that harmonizes with the delicate sweetness of the tuna. The fish, often grilled to enhance its rich flavor, is a testament to the maritime heritage of Nice.

But what truly sets the Niçoise Salad apart is the crowning glory – a perfectly poached egg. As the velvety yolk mingles with the other ingredients, it transforms the salad into a luxurious indulgence, adding a creamy texture that ties the elements together.

Pro Tip: Experience the true essence of a Niçoise Salad in a traditional bistro nestled in Old Town. Seek out places like "Le Safari" or "La Rossettisserie," where the chefs take pride in using locally sourced, seasonal ingredients.

Socca

As the sun begins its descent over the azure waters of the Mediterranean, follow your nose to the enticing aroma wafting through the air. Your olfactory senses have led you to one of Nice's most beloved street foods – Socca.

Socca, a thin pancake made from chickpea flour, is a savory delight that has been a staple in Nice for centuries. Imagine a crispy golden exterior giving way to a soft, slightly chewy interior – a textural symphony that delights with every bite.

The secret to the perfect Socca lies in the quality of chickpea flour. The local mills grind the chickpeas to perfection, ensuring a flour that imparts a distinct nuttiness to the dish. Mixed with water, olive oil, and a pinch of salt, the batter is skillfully poured onto a scorching hot copper plate.

The result is a Socca that boasts a delicate balance of flavors. The exterior, kissed by the flames, develops a subtle smokiness, while the inside remains tender and moist. It's a taste that transports you to the bustling markets of Nice, where street vendors skillfully flip Socca on massive griddles.

Pro Tip: The best Socca experience is found in the heart of Old Town at the renowned "Chez Thérésa." Join the locals in savoring this crispy delight, and pair it with a glass of chilled rosé for the perfect evening snack.

Ratatouille

As you wander through the narrow cobblestone streets of Old Town, allow the tantalizing aroma of Ratatouille to beckon you into a cozy bistro. This humble Provençal dish, though simple in its ingredients, is a symphony of flavors that encapsulates the spirit of Nice's countryside.

Ratatouille is a celebration of the region's bountiful harvest, showcasing an array of seasonal vegetables at their peak. The key players – eggplant, zucchini, bell peppers, and tomatoes – are harmoniously combined and slow-cooked to perfection.

What sets Nice's Ratatouille apart is the meticulous preparation. Each vegetable is sliced with precision, ensuring a uniform cook that preserves both texture and flavor. The dish is then infused with fragrant herbs such as thyme, rosemary, and bay leaves, providing a depth that reflects the terroir of the surrounding hills.

The result is a Ratatouille that is both rustic and refined. The vegetables, while maintaining their individuality, meld together in a symphony of flavors. The tender bites of eggplant and the slightly crisp zucchini create a delightful contrast, while the rich tomato base ties everything together.

Pro Tip: For an authentic Ratatouille experience, head to "La Trattoria" in the Port district. This hidden gem is known for its commitment to traditional Provençal flavors, offering a Ratatouille that captures the essence of Nice's countryside.

In the heart of Nice, where the azure sea meets the vibrant streets, the culinary treasures of the city await. As you savor the Niçoise Salad, Socca, and Ratatouille, remember that each bite tells a tale of tradition, craftsmanship, and the undeniable allure of the Mediterranean lifestyle. So, indulge your senses, relish the flavors, and let the culinary magic of Nice unfold before you in 2024.

Pissaladière

As the sun dips below the horizon, casting a warm glow over the Old Town, treat your taste buds to the savory delight of Pissaladière. This traditional Niçoise dish is a culinary masterpiece, featuring a thin crust topped with caramelized onions, black olives, and anchovies. The onions, slow-cooked to perfection, impart a sweet and savory flavor that perfectly complements the brininess of the olives and anchovies. Enjoy it as a starter or indulge in a slice as a delightful snack while exploring the charming streets of Old Nice.

Pro Tip: Head to "Lou Pilha Leva" in the heart of Old Town for an authentic Pissaladière experience. This local institution has been perfecting this classic dish for generations.

Pan Bagnat

As the Mediterranean breeze whispers through the palm trees, embrace the casual elegance of a Pan Bagnat. This iconic sandwich, born from the fishermen's need for a portable and hearty meal, is a symphony of flavors and textures. A round loaf of bread is generously filled with tuna, hard-boiled eggs, tomatoes, olives, and a drizzle of olive oil. The result is a handheld delight that captures the essence of a seaside picnic. Take a leisurely stroll along the Promenade des Anglais with a Pan Bagnat in hand, savoring the blend of Mediterranean goodness.

Pro Tip: For the best Pan Bagnat, head to "Socca d'Or" near the Promenade. Their commitment to using fresh, local ingredients ensures an authentic and delicious experience.

Tourte de Blette

Indulge your sweet tooth in the rustic charm of Tourte de Blette, a traditional Niçoise dessert that will transport you to a bygone era. This delectable pastry is filled with a unique combination of Swiss chard, raisins, and pine nuts, creating a sweet and savory symphony. The layers of flaky pastry cradle the flavorful filling, providing a delightful contrast in every bite. Whether enjoyed as an afternoon treat or a post-dinner dessert, Tourte de Blette is a testament to Nice's culinary diversity.

Pro Tip: Visit "Pâtisserie Canet" in Old Town for an authentic taste of Tourte de Blette. This family-owned bakery has been crafting this delightful pastry for generations.

Daube Niçoise

As the aroma of slow-cooked stew wafts through the air, discover the heartwarming flavors of Daube Niçoise. This Provençal beef stew is a comfort food classic, simmered to perfection with red wine, tomatoes, and a bouquet of aromatic herbs. The tender beef, infused with the rich flavors of the Mediterranean, melts in your mouth, creating a culinary experience that mirrors the warmth of a Niçoise embrace. Pair it with a glass of local red wine for a truly immersive taste of Nice's culinary heritage.

Pro Tip: "La Merenda," a cozy eatery tucked away in Old Town, is renowned for its authentic Daube Niçoise. Immerse yourself in the cozy atmosphere and savor this timeless dish.

Fougasse

Embark on a journey through the fragrant streets of Nice with a Fougasse in hand – a delightful bread that epitomizes the artistry of local bakers. This flatbread, adorned with various toppings like olives, herbs, or cheese, is a staple in the bakeries of Nice. The crust, golden and crispy, gives way to a soft and airy interior, creating a textural symphony that delights with every bite. Grab a Fougasse from a neighborhood boulangerie and let its flavors guide you through the hidden gems of the city.

Pro Tip: "Boulangerie Pâtisserie Béchard" in Cours Saleya is a renowned establishment for its exquisite Fougasse. Pair it with a selection of local cheeses for a true taste of the Mediterranean.

Petits Farcis

Step into the world of culinary artistry with Petits Farcis, a dish that showcases the bounty of the region's gardens. Translating to "stuffed vegetables," Petits Farcis feature a medley of zucchini, tomatoes, bell peppers, and eggplants filled with a savory stuffing of ground meat, breadcrumbs, and aromatic herbs. The vegetables, bursting with flavor, are slow-cooked to perfection, creating a dish that marries freshness with indulgence. Explore the hidden courtyards of Old Town to find a bistro that honors the tradition of Petits Farcis.

Pro Tip: "La Merenda" is renowned for its authentic Petits Farcis. Savor this dish in the quaint ambiance of the restaurant, surrounded by the echoes of centuries-old culinary craftsmanship.

Socca Pizza

Elevate your pizza experience with the local twist of Socca Pizza – a culinary innovation that fuses the beloved Socca with the world of Italian flavors. Picture a thin and crispy Socca crust, generously topped with tomato sauce, fresh mozzarella, and a medley of Mediterranean ingredients. The result is a harmonious blend of textures and tastes, where the smokiness of the Socca crust complements the richness of the toppings. Seek out artisanal pizzerias in Old Town that have embraced this fusion, offering a unique and delectable take on a global favorite.

Pro Tip: "Pisano" on Rue de la Préfecture is a hidden gem known for its Socca Pizza. Revel in the cozy atmosphere and let the flavors of this innovative creation captivate your palate.

Clafoutis Niçois

Conclude your culinary exploration with the sweet notes of Clafoutis Niçois – a dessert that encapsulates the simplicity and sophistication of Niçoise cuisine. This baked custard, enriched with local cherries and almonds, creates a luscious and indulgent treat. The magic lies in the balance of sweetness and nuttiness, with each spoonful offering a delightful interplay of flavors. Enjoy it as a decadent finale to your Niçoise dining experience, perhaps paired with a glass of Muscat wine to enhance the richness of this traditional delicacy.

Pro Tip: "Le Bistrot d'Antoine" in the Port district is celebrated for its Clafoutis Niçois. Indulge in the elegant ambiance and savor the velvety textures of this dessert as you bid adieu to the flavors of Nice.

In the heart of Nice, where culinary traditions are woven into the fabric of daily life, these additional delicacies beckon you to explore the diverse tapestry of flavors that define the city's gastronomic landscape in 2024. Each bite is an invitation to embark on a sensory journey, a testament to the rich culinary heritage that awaits those who venture into the charming streets and hidden corners of Nice. So, let your palate guide you through this gastronomic odyssey, where every dish tells a story of passion, tradition, and the everlasting allure of the Mediterranean.

Restaurants and Cafés

Fine Dining

1. Le Chantecler

Experience the Pinnacle of French Gastronomy

- Immerse yourself in the opulence of Le Chantecler, located within the historic Hotel Negresco. Indulge in a symphony of flavors orchestrated by Executive Chef Virginie Basselot, a Michelin-starred culinary virtuoso. The menu, a masterpiece of French cuisine, features delicacies like truffle-infused foie gras and lobster medallions. The extensive wine list ensures a perfect pairing for every dish, enhancing your gastronomic journey.

- Address: 37 Promenade des Anglais, 06000 Nice, France
- Phone: +33 4 93 16 64 00
- Opening Hours: Tuesday-Saturday (7:30 PM - 10:00 PM)
- Price Range: $150 - $300 per person

2. Jan

- A Culinary Oasis with a South African Twist
- Discover the culinary magic at Jan, where Michelin-starred Chef Jan Hendrik invites you to a gastronomic adventure influenced by his South African roots. Savor dishes like smoked springbok and rooibos-infused desserts in an intimate and art-filled setting. The seasonal menu ensures freshness and creativity, making Jan a top choice for discerning palates.
- Address: 12 Rue Lascaris, 06300 Nice, France
- Phone: +33 4 97 19 32 23
- Opening Hours: Wednesday-Saturday (7:00 PM - 10:00 PM)
- Price Range: $120 - $250 per person

3. La Petite Maison

Mediterranean Elegance with a Dash of Riviera Charm

- La Petite Maison captures the essence of Mediterranean dining with a focus on fresh, high-quality ingredients. Renowned for its vibrant atmosphere, this restaurant offers a menu featuring signature dishes like grilled sea bass and marinated lamb cutlets. Immerse yourself in the lively ambiance while relishing the flavors of the French Riviera.
- Address: 11 Rue Saint-François de Paule, 06300 Nice, France

- Phone: +33 4 93 92 59 59
- Opening Hours: Daily (12:00 PM - 3:00 PM, 7:00 PM - 11:00 PM)
- Price Range: $80 - $150 per person

4. Keisuke Matsushima

Japanese-French Fusion Excellence

- Elevate your dining experience at Keisuke Matsushima, a culinary gem blending Japanese precision with French flair. Chef Matsushima's innovative creations, like miso-glazed black cod and sushi-inspired foie gras, showcase a fusion of flavors. The minimalist yet stylish ambiance adds to the overall sophistication of this Michelin-starred establishment.
- Address: 22 Rue de France, 06000 Nice, France
- Phone: +33 4 93 82 26 06
- Opening Hours: Tuesday-Saturday (12:00 PM - 1:30 PM, 7:30 PM - 9:30 PM)
- Price Range: $90 - $200 per person

5. L'Univers

Historical Charm with Culinary Excellence

- Immerse yourself in the historic surroundings of L'Univers, a gastronomic institution in Nice since 1829. With its Belle Époque décor, this restaurant offers classic French dishes prepared with a contemporary twist. From escargot to duck confit, L'Univers invites you to savor the timeless flavors of traditional French cuisine in an elegant and storied setting.
- Address: 2 Rue de la Liberté, 06300 Nice, France
- Phone: +33 4 93 85 77 98

- Opening Hours: Monday-Saturday (12:00 PM - 2:00 PM, 7:30 PM - 10:00 PM)
- Price Range: $70 - $120 per person

Casual Eateries

1. Lou Pilha Leva

A Charming Local Bistro with a Provençal Soul

- Embrace the warmth of Provençal hospitality at Lou Pilha Leva, a hidden gem known for its authentic Niçois cuisine. From socca to pissaladière, each dish reflects the flavors of the region. The laid-back ambiance and outdoor seating make it an ideal spot for a leisurely lunch or dinner, providing a true taste of Nice's culinary heritage.
- Address: 10 Rue du Collet, 06300 Nice, France
- Phone: +33 4 93 80 72 49
- Opening Hours: Monday-Saturday (12:00 PM - 2:30 PM, 7:00 PM - 10:00 PM)
- Price Range: $20 - $40 per person

2. Chez Pipo

Savor the Best Socca in Town

- A local favorite, Chez Pipo has been serving mouthwatering socca since 1923. This casual eatery exudes a friendly, communal atmosphere, making it a cherished spot for both locals and visitors. Order a plate of socca, a chickpea pancake, and pair it with a glass of local rosé for an authentic Niçois culinary experience.
- Address: 13 Rue Bavastro, 06300 Nice, France

- Phone: +33 4 93 55 88 82
- Opening Hours: Tuesday-Saturday (12:00 PM - 2:30 PM, 7:00 PM - 9:30 PM)
- Price Range: $15 - $25 per person

3. La Merenda

A Homage to Traditional Niçois Cuisine

- Step into the rustic charm of La Merenda, a small bistro celebrated for its dedication to preserving Niçois culinary traditions. The ever-changing menu features regional specialties like stuffed vegetables and daube (beef stew). The intimate setting and limited seating create an authentic and communal dining experience.
- Address: 4 Rue Raoul Bosio, 06300 Nice, France
- Phone: +33 4 93 85 29 57
- Opening Hours: Monday-Friday (12:00 PM - 2:00 PM, 7:00 PM - 9:00 PM)
- Price Range: $25 - $50 per person

4. Bistrot d'Antoine

Modern Twist on Classic French Bistro Fare
- Bistrot d'Antoine seamlessly blends the old and the new, offering a contemporary take on traditional French bistro cuisine. Enjoy dishes like duck confit and coq au vin in a relaxed setting adorned with vintage memorabilia. The diverse menu and friendly ambiance make it a go-to spot for those seeking a casual yet elevated dining experience.
- Address: 27 Rue de la Préfecture, 06300 Nice, France
- Phone: +33 4 93 85 29 57
- Opening Hours: Tuesday-Sunday (12:00 PM - 2:30 PM, 7:00 PM - 10:30 PM)

- Price Range: $30 - $60 per person

5. Acchiardo

A Family Legacy of Flavors

- Acchiardo, a family-run establishment since 1927, invites you to experience authentic Niçois cuisine in a cozy and welcoming atmosphere. From seafood to hearty stews, each dish reflects the culinary heritage passed down through generations. The handwritten menu adds a personal touch, making your dining experience a journey through the heart of Nice's gastronomic traditions.
- Address: 38 Rue Droite, 06300 Nice, France
- Phone: +33 4 93 85 51 16
- Opening Hours: Monday-Saturday (12:00 PM - 2:30 PM, 7:00 PM - 10:00 PM)
- Price Range: $25 - $45 per person

Waterfront Dining

1. Le Plongeoir

Romantic Seaside Dining at its Finest

- Perched on a rocky outcrop overlooking the Mediterranean, Le Plongeoir offers a unique and romantic waterfront dining experience. With waves gently lapping beneath your feet, relish a seafood-centric menu featuring oysters and grilled fish. The intimate setting, enhanced by the sea breeze, makes it an ideal spot for a special evening.
- Address: 60 Boulevard Franck Pilatte, 06300 Nice, France
- Phone: +33 4 93 26 53 02

- Opening Hours: Daily (12:00 PM - 3:00 PM, 7:00 PM - 10:00 PM)
- Price Range: $80 - $150 per person

2. La Voglia

Italian Delights with a Sea View
- Enjoy the fusion of Italian and Mediterranean flavors at La Voglia, located along the Promenade des Anglais. The terrace, offering panoramic views of the sea, sets the stage for a delightful dining experience. Indulge in handmade pasta and fresh seafood dishes while basking in the golden hues of the sunset.
- Address: 2 Quai des États-Unis, 06300 Nice, France
- Phone: +33 4 93 87 28 34
- Opening Hours: Daily (12:00 PM - 2:30 PM, 7:00 PM - 10:30 PM)
- Price Range: $60 - $120 per person

3. Castel Plage

Beachfront Elegance with Mediterranean Cuisine

- Castel Plage, nestled on the iconic Promenade des Anglais, offers a sophisticated beachfront dining experience. Sink your toes in the sand while savoring dishes like grilled sea bass and Provencal salad. The chic atmosphere and attentive service make it a perfect spot for a leisurely lunch or a romantic dinner under the stars.
- Address: 8 Quai des États-Unis, 06000 Nice, France
- Phone: +33 4 93 85 22 66
- Opening Hours: Daily (9:00 AM - 12:00 AM)
- Price Range: $70 - $130 per person

4. Le Bistrot de la Mer

Seafood Paradise with a Relaxed Atmosphere

- Immerse yourself in the maritime charm of Le Bistrot de la Mer, a laid-back eatery overlooking the Old Port. Feast on a menu featuring the freshest catch of the day, from grilled sardines to seafood platters. The casual ambiance and panoramic sea views create a perfect setting for a seafood-centric dining experience.
- Address: 5 Quai des Deux Emmanuel, 06300 Nice, France
- Phone: +33 4 93 56 00 36
- Opening Hours: Daily (12:00 PM - 3:00 PM, 7:00 PM - 10:00 PM)
- Price Range: $50 - $100 per person

5. Le Galet

A Culinary Gem on the Water's Edge

- Nestled on the rocks of the Baie des Anges, Le Galet offers a unique dining experience where the sea becomes an extension of the restaurant. Delight in a menu showcasing Mediterranean flavors, including bouillabaisse and grilled octopus. The rhythmic sound of the waves and the sea breeze create a magical ambiance for an unforgettable meal.
- Address: 2 Boulevard Franck Pilatte, 06300 Nice, France
- Phone: +33 4 93 80 06 27
- Opening Hours: Daily (12:00 PM - 3:00 PM, 7:00 PM - 10:00 PM)
- Price Range: $90 - $160 per person

Indulge in the diverse culinary offerings of Nice, each venue promising a unique blend of flavors and atmospheres.

Whether you seek refined elegance, casual charm, or the romance of seaside dining, the restaurants and cafés of Nice invite you to savor the essence of the French Riviera.

VI. Shopping in Nice

Markets and Bazaars

Cours Saleya Market

Welcome to the Heartbeat of Nice's Culinary Scene

Nestled in the heart of Old Town, the Cours Saleya Market is an epicenter of sights, scents, and flavors that define the essence of Nice. This vibrant market operates every day except Monday when it transforms into a captivating antique market. Get ready to immerse yourself in the lively atmosphere, where local vendors display an array of fresh produce, flowers, and artisanal products.

Location:
Cours Saleya, 06300 Nice, France

Contact Information:
Phone: +33 4 93 62 60 67

Opening Hours:

Tuesday to Sunday: 6:00 AM - 5:30 PM
Monday (Antique Market): 7:00 AM - 6:00 PM

Highlights:

Fresh Produce Stalls: Start your day by exploring the vivid array of fresh fruits, vegetables, and aromatic herbs. Engage with local vendors, who are more than happy to share insights on their produce.

Flower Market: Surround yourself with the fragrant blooms of the Flower Market. Admire the vivid colors of locally grown flowers, and perhaps find a bouquet to brighten your accommodations.

Delightful Delicacies: Indulge in local delicacies such as socca (chickpea flatbread), pan bagnat (a Nicoise sandwich), and artisanal cheeses. Don't forget to pair these treats with a glass of regional wine for the full experience.

Tips for Maximizing Your Visit:

Early Bird Advantage: Visit the market early to avoid crowds and secure the freshest produce.

Negotiate with a Smile: Many vendors are open to friendly negotiations, so don't hesitate to strike up a conversation and potentially snag a deal.

Monday Antique Market: If your visit coincides with a Monday, explore the antique market for unique finds and vintage treasures.

Liberation Market

Unlocking the Local Flavors of Liberation

For a more local and authentic shopping experience, Liberation Market stands out as a hidden gem in the bustling Liberation neighborhood. Here, you'll discover a mix of traditional French products and a diverse range of international offerings. Liberation Market captures the essence of daily life in Nice, making it a favorite among locals seeking high-quality ingredients.

Location:
Place du Général de Gaulle, 06000 Nice, France

Contact Information:
Phone: +33 4 93 13 31 31

Opening Hours:

Tuesday to Sunday: 7:00 AM - 1:00 PM
Closed on Mondays

Highlights:

Fresh Seafood: Dive into the world of Mediterranean cuisine with the market's seafood stalls. From fresh catches to exotic specialties, the seafood selection is a gastronomic delight.

Local Cheeses and Charcuterie: Delve into the rich world of French cheeses and cured meats. Let the vendors guide you through their offerings, providing samples and pairing suggestions.

International Flavors: Liberation Market reflects Nice's multicultural atmosphere. Explore stalls featuring spices, olives, and specialties from around the world.

Tips for Maximizing Your Visit:

Tasting Opportunities: Vendors often offer tastings, so take advantage of this to discover new flavors and find your favorites.

BYOB - Bring Your Own Bag: Embrace eco-friendly practices by bringing your reusable bag to carry your market finds.

Morning Excursion: Plan your visit in the morning to witness the market at its liveliest and to enjoy the freshest products.

Embark on a culinary journey through these markets, and let the local flavors of Cours Saleya and Liberation Market become the highlight of your visit to Nice. These markets not only offer a feast for your senses but also provide a window into the authentic daily life and rich cultural tapestry of this enchanting city.

Fashion and Souvenirs

Avenue Jean Médecin

Where Style Meets Tradition

Avenue Jean Médecin, often referred to as Nice's shopping paradise, is the beating heart of the city's fashion scene. Stretching from Place Masséna to the railway station, this grand boulevard is lined with a diverse array of shops, boutiques, and department stores. From international brands to local designers, Avenue Jean Médecin offers a shopping experience that seamlessly blends contemporary trends with the city's traditional elegance.

Location:
Avenue Jean Médecin, 06000 Nice, France

Contact Information:
No specific contact information, as it's a public street.

Shopping Hours:

Most shops open from 10:00 AM to 7:00 PM (may vary by store)

Highlights:

Galeries Lafayette: Dive into the world of high-end fashion at Galeries Lafayette. Explore the latest collections from renowned designers and enjoy a sophisticated shopping environment.

Nice Étoile Shopping Center: This multi-story shopping center is a haven for fashion enthusiasts. Discover a mix of international and local brands, as well as cafes for a quick shopping break.

Local Boutiques: Venture into charming local boutiques scattered along the avenue. Here, you can find unique pieces crafted by local designers, offering a true taste of Nice's fashion culture.

Tips for Maximizing Your Visit:

Window Shopping: Even if you're not planning on a shopping spree, take a leisurely stroll down the avenue to enjoy the vibrant atmosphere and stunning architecture.

Midweek Advantage: Visit during weekdays for a more relaxed shopping experience, as weekends tend to draw larger crowds.

Café Culture: Embrace the French tradition of café culture. Take a break at one of the street-side cafes, sip on a coffee, and watch the world go by.

Old Town Boutiques

Discovering Unique Treasures in Vieux Nice

For a more intimate and eclectic shopping experience, venture into the narrow, winding streets of Old Town. Here, boutique shopping takes on a whole new meaning, with charming stores offering handmade crafts, vintage finds, and locally inspired souvenirs. Each boutique tells a story, making your shopping excursion a journey into the soul of Nice's artistic and cultural heritage.

Location:
Vieux Nice (Old Town), 06300 Nice, France

Contact Information:
Varies by boutique; inquire within each store.

Shopping Hours:

Typically from 10:00 AM to 7:00 PM, but may vary by boutique.
Highlights:

Fenocchio: Indulge your sweet tooth at Fenocchio, a legendary ice cream parlor offering a staggering variety of flavors. It's not just ice cream; it's a Nice tradition.

Artisanal Craft Shops: Explore boutiques showcasing handmade crafts, ceramics, and artwork by local artisans. Purchase a unique piece to take home as a lasting memory of your trip.

Vintage Finds: Scour vintage shops for one-of-a-kind fashion pieces, antique trinkets, and retro treasures. Unearth hidden gems that tell the tales of bygone eras.

Tips for Maximizing Your Visit:

Curiosity Pays: Don't be afraid to wander off the main streets. Some of the most charming boutiques are tucked away in the quieter corners of Old Town.

Cultural Connections: Engage with boutique owners, many of whom are passionate about their craft. Learn about the stories behind the products for a richer shopping experience.

Evening Charm: Old Town takes on a magical ambiance in the evening. Consider extending your shopping adventure into the night to enjoy the romantic atmosphere.

Immerse yourself in the world of fashion and unique finds as you explore the chic offerings of Avenue Jean Médecin and the hidden treasures within the boutiques of Old Town. These shopping destinations are not just about acquiring material possessions; they are gateways to the soul of Nice, each offering a unique perspective on the city's rich cultural tapestry.

VII. Entertainment and Nightlife

Evening Activities

1. Promenade Walks

Promenade des Anglais:
Start your evening with a leisurely stroll along the iconic Promenade des Anglais. As the sun sets, the vibrant colors paint the sky, creating a breathtaking backdrop. This world-famous promenade stretches along the azure waters of the Mediterranean Sea, offering a perfect setting for a romantic evening or a casual walk with friends.

- Address: Promenade des Anglais, 06000 Nice, France
- Opening Hours: Always open

Tip: Grab a delicious gelato from one of the nearby vendors and enjoy the view from one of the iconic blue chairs lining the promenade. Sunset is particularly magical.

Castle Hill (Colline du Château):
For a more elevated experience, head to Castle Hill, providing panoramic views of the city and the bay. The walk up may be a bit steep, but the stunning scenery and the old ruins at the top make it worthwhile. This is an ideal spot to witness the city lights sparkling as the night unfolds.

- Address: Colline du Château, 06300 Nice, France
- Contact: N/A
- Opening Hours: 8:00 AM - 6:00 PM (Varies seasonally)

Tip: Bring a picnic and enjoy a sunset dinner with a view. The ambiance is truly magical as the city lights start to twinkle.

Old Town (Vieux Nice):
Explore the narrow cobblestone streets of Old Town during the evening, where the atmosphere transforms into a lively hub of activity. With its charming architecture, vibrant markets, and cozy cafes, this area exudes a unique charm as dusk settles over Nice.

- Address: Vieux Nice, 06300 Nice, France
- Opening Hours: Most shops and restaurants open until 10:00 PM

Tip: Visit Place Rossetti for a taste of local ice cream or join the locals in one of the bustling pubs for a refreshing drink.

Promenade du Paillon:
If you prefer a more urban setting, take a walk through the Promenade du Paillon. This beautifully landscaped park in the heart of Nice features water fountains, modern sculptures, and inviting green spaces. Lit up at night, it offers a serene yet lively environment.

- Address: Promenade du Paillon, 06300 Nice, France
- Opening Hours: Always open

Tip: Check the schedule for any evening events or performances taking place in the park. It's a great spot for a relaxing evening surrounded by nature.

Mont Boron:
For a less crowded but equally captivating experience, venture to Mont Boron. This hillside area provides stunning views of the city lights reflecting on the Mediterranean. The serenity of the location makes it an ideal spot for a romantic evening or a peaceful solo walk.

- Address: Mont Boron, 06300 Nice, France
- Opening Hours: Always open

Tip: Bring a blanket and some snacks for a quiet evening picnic. The ambiance here is tranquil, away from the hustle and bustle of the city.

2. Live Performances

Théâtre de la Photographie et de l'Image:
Immerse yourself in the world of visual arts and live performances at Théâtre de la Photographie et de l'Image. This cultural space hosts a variety of events, including photography exhibitions, film screenings, and live performances. Check their schedule for upcoming shows during your visit.

- Address: 27 Boulevard Dubouchage, 06000 Nice, France
- Contact: +33 4 97 13 42 20
- Opening Hours: 10:00 AM - 6:00 PM (Closed on Mondays)
- Upcoming Events: Theatre Nice Events

Tip: Arrive early to explore the current exhibitions before enjoying a live performance. The intimate setting adds to the overall artistic experience.

Opéra de Nice:
Indulge in the grandeur of classical music and opera at the Opéra de Nice. This historic venue, with its ornate architecture, hosts a range of performances, from timeless operas to contemporary ballets. Check their schedule for a cultural evening filled with elegance.

- Address: 4-6 Rue Saint-François de Paule, 06300 Nice, France

- Contact: +33 4 92 17 40 79
- Box Office Hours: 10:00 AM - 6:00 PM (Closed on Sundays)

Upcoming Performances: Opéra de Nice Schedule

Tip: Opt for a guided tour of the opera house during the day to appreciate its architectural beauty before attending an evening performance.

Théâtre National de Nice:

For a taste of contemporary theater and avant-garde performances, head to the Théâtre National de Nice. This dynamic venue showcases a diverse range of theatrical productions, from cutting-edge plays to experimental performances.

- Address: 1 Promenade des Arts, 06300 Nice, France
- Contact: +33 4 93 13 90 90
- Box Office Hours: 11:00 AM - 6:00 PM (Closed on Mondays)
- Upcoming Shows: TN Nice Agenda

Tip: Consider booking tickets in advance, especially for popular shows. The theater's modern design enhances the overall viewing experience.

Jazz Clubs in Old Town:

For a more laid-back yet culturally rich evening, explore the jazz clubs in Old Town. These intimate venues often feature local musicians, creating a cozy atmosphere for jazz enthusiasts and those looking to discover the soulful sounds of Nice.

- Address: Various locations in Old Town, Nice, France
- Contact: Check individual club listings
- Opening Hours: Varies by venue

Tip: Ask locals for recommendations or explore different clubs in one evening to get a taste of the diverse jazz scene in Nice.

Promenade du Paillon Concerts:
Experience the joy of live music in an outdoor setting by checking out concerts held at Promenade du Paillon. The park occasionally hosts musical events, ranging from classical performances to contemporary bands. Pack a picnic and enjoy an evening of music under the stars.

- Address: Promenade du Paillon, 06300 Nice, France
- Contact: Check local event listings
- Opening Hours: Varies by event

Tip: Follow local event calendars or ask at the tourist information center for upcoming concerts. Arrive early to secure a good spot for your blanket or chair.

Embark on these evening activities, and you'll discover the true essence of Nice's charm as it comes alive under the enchanting glow of the moon and city lights.

Bars and Nightclubs

Old Town Pubs

Ma Nolan's Irish Pub

Nestled in the heart of Old Town, Ma Nolan's Irish Pub is a vibrant establishment that seamlessly blends the warmth of traditional Irish pubs with the Mediterranean spirit of Nice. The cozy interiors and friendly atmosphere make it a favorite among locals and visitors alike. Enjoy live music performances and a vast selection of Irish and local beers. The pub also serves hearty pub grub, perfect for a casual evening out.

- Address: 2 Rue Saint-François de Paule, 06300 Nice, France
- Phone: +33 4 93 92 18 18
- Opening Hours: Monday to Sunday, 11:00 AM to 2:00 AM
- Average Cost: $20-$30 per person for food and drinks
- Amenities: Live Music, Outdoor Seating, Sports Screenings
- Website: www.manolans.com

Wayne's Bar

Tucked away in a narrow alley, Wayne's Bar exudes a hip and trendy vibe. This local gem is known for its extensive cocktail menu and skilled mixologists. The intimate setting is perfect for a date night or catching up with friends. Try their signature cocktails and soak in the artistic décor that adds to the overall experience.

- Address: 15 Rue de la Préfecture, 06300 Nice, France
- Phone: +33 6 22 17 97 07
- Opening Hours: Tuesday to Sunday, 6:00 PM to 2:00 AM
- Average Cost: $12-$15 per cocktail
- Amenities: Craft Cocktails, Cozy Ambiance
- Website: www.waynesbar.com

The Snug

For those seeking an authentic English pub experience, The Snug in Old Town is the place to be. With its wooden interiors, dartboards, and a selection of English ales, it's a home away from home for expats and tourists alike. Don't miss their Sunday roast for a taste of traditional British comfort food.

- Address: 22 Rue de la Préfecture, 06300 Nice, France
- Phone: +33 4 93 80 37 67
- Opening Hours: Monday to Sunday, 12:00 PM to 2:00 AM
- Average Cost: $15-$25 per person for food and drinks
- Amenities: Dartboards, English Ales, Sunday Roast
- Website: www.thesnugnice.com

Les Distilleries Idéales

Situated in a charming square, Les Distilleries Idéales is a French pub known for its extensive selection of craft beers and spirits. The outdoor seating provides a perfect spot for people-watching. The pub's knowledgeable staff can guide you through their impressive menu, ensuring you find the perfect drink to suit your taste.

- Address: 24 Rue de la Préfecture, 06300 Nice, France
- Phone: +33 4 93 85 99 47
- Opening Hours: Tuesday to Sunday, 5:00 PM to 2:00 AM
- Average Cost: $8-$12 per drink
- Amenities: Outdoor Seating, Craft Beers, Spirits
- Website: www.lesdistilleriesideales.com

Le Bistrot d'Antoine

Blending the charm of a French bistro with the conviviality of a pub, Le Bistrot d'Antoine is a local favorite. Known for its extensive wine list and delicious small plates, it's a great place to start your evening. The laid-back ambiance and friendly staff make it an ideal spot for winding down after a day of exploring.

- Address: 27 Rue de la Préfecture, 06300 Nice, France
- Phone: +33 4 93 85 29 57
- Opening Hours: Monday to Sunday, 5:00 PM to 2:00 AM
- Average Cost: $25-$40 per person for wine and tapas
- Amenities: Extensive Wine List, Small Plates
- Website: www.lebistrotdantoine.com

Closing Note: To fully immerse yourself in the vibrant atmosphere of Old Town, consider exploring these pubs during the early evening or late afternoon. Each pub has its unique charm, so don't hesitate to try a different one each night for a diverse experience. Always check for special events or live performances for an added touch of local entertainment.

Promenade Lounges

Le Méridien Nice - Rooftop Lounge Bar

Perched on the top of Le Méridien Nice, this rooftop lounge bar offers breathtaking panoramic views of the Mediterranean Sea and the city. Indulge in creative cocktails and tapas while lounging in a stylish and sophisticated setting. Sunset hours are particularly magical, creating a memorable ambiance.

- Address: 1 Promenade des Anglais, 06046 Nice, France
- Phone: +33 4 97 03 44 44
- Opening Hours: Monday to Sunday, 5:00 PM to 1:00 AM
- Average Cost: $20-$30 per cocktail
- Amenities: Rooftop Views, Creative Cocktails, Tapas
- Website: www.lemeridiennice.com

Sky Beach

For a laid-back and beachy atmosphere, Sky Beach on the Promenade des Anglais is a fantastic choice. Sink into comfortable lounge chairs on the sandy terrace while sipping on refreshing cocktails. The cool sea breeze and the sound of the waves create a relaxed ambiance, perfect for unwinding.

- Address: 59 Promenade des Anglais, 06000 Nice, France
- Phone: +33 4 97 03 89 89
- Opening Hours: Tuesday to Sunday, 10:00 AM to 12:00 AM
- Average Cost: $15-$25 per cocktail
- Amenities: Beachfront, Lounge Chairs, Cocktails
- Website: www.skybeach.fr

Le Plongeoir

Literally translating to "The Diving Board," Le Plongeoir offers a unique and upscale lounge experience on a converted diving board over the Mediterranean. Enjoy exclusive cocktails and a Mediterranean-inspired menu while surrounded by the sparkling sea. Reservations are recommended for this one-of-a-kind venue.

- Address: 60 Boulevard Franck Pilatte, 06300 Nice, France
- Phone: +33 4 93 01 32 10
- Opening Hours: Wednesday to Sunday, 11:00 AM to 12:00 AM
- Average Cost: $30-$50 per person for cocktails and snacks
- Amenities: Exclusive Lounge, Sea Views, Mediterranean Menu
- Website: www.leplongeoir.com

L'Effervescence

Situated on the Promenade des Anglais, L'Effervescence offers a chic and sophisticated lounge experience. With a curated selection of champagne and expertly crafted cocktails, this venue is ideal for those seeking an elegant evening. The modern décor and attentive service contribute to a memorable night out.

- Address: 39 Promenade des Anglais, 06000 Nice, France
- Phone: +33 6 64 22 75 68
- Opening Hours: Monday to Sunday, 5:00 PM to 2:00 AM
- Average Cost: $25-$40 per drink
- Amenities: Champagne Selection, Modern Decor, Terrace
- Website: www.leffervescence-nice.fr

Le Sansas

Nestled near the Port of Nice, Le Sansas offers a laid-back lounge atmosphere with a focus on local and artisanal products. The terrace provides stunning views of the harbor and the city lights. Enjoy their signature cocktails and a selection of Mediterranean-inspired snacks in a relaxed setting.

- Address: 13 Quai des Deux Emmanuel, 06300 Nice, France
- Phone: +33 6 01 73 74 58
- Opening Hours: Tuesday to Sunday, 6:00 PM to 1:00 AM
- Average Cost: $18-$25 per cocktail
- Amenities: Harbor Views, Artisanal Products, Terrace
- Website: www.lesansas-nice.fr

Closing Note: Promenade lounges offer a diverse range of experiences, from the glamorous rooftop settings to the laid-back beachfront vibes. Plan your visit during the early evening to witness the sunset and transition into a sophisticated night of leisure. Reservations are advisable for exclusive venues like Le Plongeoir.

VIII. Practical Information

Currency and Money Matters

Money, ah, that essential companion on your journey. As you step into the sun-kissed streets of Nice, having a handle on the local currency and money nuances is key to a seamless adventure. The currency of the realm is the Euro (EUR), a currency that embodies the elegance of the French Riviera. While credit cards are widely accepted, it's wise to carry some cash for those charming, tucked-away shops or street vendors in the Old Town.

Venture into the heart of Nice's financial scene with Avenue Jean Médecin, where banks and exchange bureaus dance along the boulevard. Here, indulge in a bit of retail therapy at Galeries Lafayette, and conveniently sort out your currency needs in one fell swoop. Keep an eye out for those hidden gems in the boutiques of Old Town, where cash can sometimes be the golden key to unlocking unique finds.

And speaking of finds, consider exploring Liberation Market for a sensory journey through local flavors. Your pocket change transforms into an entrance ticket to a cornucopia of fresh produce and artisanal treats. Engaging with local vendors in their preferred currency can open doors to delightful conversations and, who knows, perhaps a few extra smiles with your purchases.

Language Tips

Now, let's dive into the poetic symphony that is the French language. While many locals speak English, a sprinkle of basic French phrases can be the magic wand that opens doors and hearts. "Bonjour" is your golden ticket to a friendly exchange, and a heartfelt "Merci" goes a long way, especially when you've just savored a mouthwatering Niçoise Salad.

As you wander the narrow lanes of Old Town, don't be shy to practice your "Excusez-moi" when navigating the bustling markets. Embrace the rhythm of the local dialect, and watch as doors are effortlessly opened for you, revealing the true essence of Niçois hospitality.

For an immersive linguistic experience, venture beyond the tourist-heavy areas and strike up conversations with the locals in the charming cafes of Cours Saleya. You'll find that attempting a few words in French not only enriches your travel experience but also earns you a nod of appreciation from the locals, turning a simple transaction into a cultural exchange.

Safety Tips

Safety, the silent guardian of your travel narrative. Nice, with its enchanting beauty, is generally considered safe, but a sprinkle of caution never hurt anyone. Keep a vigilant eye on your belongings, especially in crowded areas like the vibrant Old Town markets. The art of pickpocketing is an unfortunate reality, but a well-worn money belt or a secure crossbody bag can be your trusty sidekick in navigating the city unscathed.

When exploring the nightlife, stick to well-lit and populated areas, and opt for reputable transportation options when navigating the city after dark. While the city sleeps, the charm of Nice awakens, but it's essential to remain aware of your surroundings.

Engage with fellow travelers and locals for insider tips on the safest routes and neighborhoods. Platforms like local forums or even a friendly chat with your hotel concierge can provide invaluable insights into navigating Nice with confidence, ensuring that your travel memoir is filled with joyous tales rather than cautionary notes.

Useful Apps and Resources

In this digital age, your smartphone is your compass, and a few well-chosen apps can elevate your Nice experience. Start your journey with the official Nice Travel Guide app, a local gem that unveils the city's secrets and guides you through its historical tapestry. From audio walking tours to interactive maps, this app is your virtual companion, decoding the city's nuances with finesse.

When conquering the culinary landscape, TripAdvisor becomes your Michelin guide in the palm of your hand. Dive into the reviews, discover hidden bistros, and share your own gastronomic adventures with fellow travelers.

For seamless navigation, CityMapper is the unsung hero of your exploration. With real-time transit updates and detailed route planning, it transforms the city into your personal playground. Combine this with the local bike-sharing app, Vélo Bleu, and you'll effortlessly pedal through Nice's scenic vistas, embracing the city at your own pace.

As the sun sets and the stars dot the Riviera sky, Shazam becomes your musical confidante. Uncover the soulful tunes echoing through the streets, creating a bespoke soundtrack for your journey.

Navigating the city is a breeze when you're prepared for the atmospheric symphony of Nice. Leverage weather apps like AccuWeather or Windy to stay ahead of the climate curve. Whether you're planning a leisurely stroll along the Promenade des Anglais or a day trip to the nearby coastal towns, these apps provide real-time forecasts, ensuring that your adventures are not dampened by unexpected weather whims.

For the language enthusiast within you, Duolingo transforms your spare moments into French lessons. Brush up on your conversational skills, master essential phrases, and embark on a linguistic journey that transcends the typical tourist experience. Imagine the joy when you seamlessly order your morning croissant or engage in a brief chat with a local artist in their native tongue.

Navigate Nice with a touch of eco-friendly flair by hopping onto an electric scooter. The Nice Ride app allows you to locate and unlock e-scooters scattered across the city. Zip through the streets, discovering hidden corners and scenic viewpoints with the wind in your hair. It's not just a mode of transport; it's a fun and efficient way to weave through the tapestry of Nice.

For an extra layer of cultural immersion, Culture Trip is your digital passport to local insights. From off-the-beaten-path attractions to hidden gems in the city's artistic tapestry, this app provides curated articles and recommendations from local experts. Discover the stories behind the landmarks, uncovering the living history that makes Nice more than just a picturesque postcard.

In the age of digital storytelling, don't forget the charm of sending and receiving postcards. With Postagram, turn your favorite travel snapshots into tangible postcards that can be sent to your loved ones with a personalized message. It's a delightful way to share the magic of Nice and immortalize your experiences in a tangible form.

Before you even set foot in Nice, tune into The Earful Tower, a Paris-based podcast that delves into the intricacies of

French culture and language. While not specifically focused on Nice, it provides a valuable backdrop to understanding the broader French context. Gain insights into cultural nuances, and let the anecdotes shared on the podcast color your experience as you explore the vibrant streets of Nice.

In this age of information, harnessing the power of these apps and resources ensures that every moment in Nice is maximized, leaving you with a travelogue that reads like a symphony of experiences, a crescendo of memories that will linger long after the echoes of your footsteps have faded from the cobblestone streets.

IX. Events and Festivals in 2024

Annual Highlights

Nice Carnival

Welcome to the vibrant and enchanting world of Nice Carnival, a spectacle that graces the city with a burst of color, music, and contagious energy. Taking place annually in February, the Nice Carnival is a celebration deeply rooted in tradition and creativity. The streets come alive with giant floats, masked parades, and lively music, making it one of the largest carnivals globally.

Experience the Carnival Magic:

Parade of Floats: Kick off your Carnival experience by immersing yourself in the spectacular parades featuring intricate and larger-than-life floats. These artistic creations showcase the incredible craftsmanship and creativity of the locals.

Flower Battles: Don't miss the iconic Bataille de Fleurs, or Flower Battle, where flower-covered floats glide through the streets, and participants throw flowers to the crowd. It's a floral fantasy that fills the air with the sweet scent of blossoms.

Carnival Parties: Join the lively street parties that spill into the night, with locals and tourists alike dancing to the rhythm of live music. Explore the Old Town during the Carnival nights to discover pop-up bars and lively gatherings.

Practical Information:

Dates: The Nice Carnival typically takes place in February, with exact dates varying each year. Check the official website for the most up-to-date information.

Cost: While street events are often free, tickets for grandstand seating during parades and certain events range from $20 to $100.

Tips: Arrive early to secure a good spot for the parades. Wear comfortable shoes as you might find yourself dancing in the streets until the wee hours.

Nice Jazz Festival

Jazz enthusiasts, get ready for a musical journey like no other at the Nice Jazz Festival. Held annually in July, this event transforms the city into a haven for music lovers, drawing international artists and creating an atmosphere pulsating with rhythm and soul.

Immerse Yourself in the Jazz Vibe:

Diverse Lineup: From classic jazz to contemporary fusion, the Nice Jazz Festival boasts a diverse lineup that caters to all musical tastes. Enjoy performances by renowned artists as well as emerging talents.

Open-Air Venues: Picture this – balmy summer nights, a starlit sky, and the soulful sounds of jazz filling the air. The festival utilizes open-air venues, such as the stunning Place Masséna, creating a unique and unforgettable experience.

Workshops and Masterclasses: Dive deeper into the world of jazz by participating in workshops and masterclasses offered during the festival. Interact with musicians, learn about improvisation, and gain insights into the artistry behind the music.

Practical Information:

Dates: The Nice Jazz Festival usually spans several days in July. Check the official website for specific dates and the lineup.

Cost: Ticket prices vary depending on the artist lineup and seating options, ranging from $30 to $150.

Tips: Bring a picnic blanket to comfortably enjoy the open-air concerts. Check the schedule in advance to plan your preferred performances and explore the city during the day.

Bastille Day Celebrations

Experience the grandeur of Bastille Day, France's National Day, in the heart of Nice every July 14th. The city transforms into a patriotic spectacle with military parades, colorful fireworks lighting up the night sky, and an infectious sense of national pride.

Celebrate Liberty, Equality, and Fraternity:

Military Parade: Begin your day by witnessing the impressive military parade along the Promenade des Anglais. Marvel at precision drills, impressive flyovers, and the display of French military prowess.

Fireworks Extravaganza: As the sun sets, head to the beach for a dazzling fireworks display. The Baie des Anges becomes a canvas for a pyrotechnic masterpiece, celebrating the values of the French Republic.

Street Parties: Join locals and tourists alike in the lively street parties that continue into the night. Share in the joy of the French spirit, dance to live music, and indulge in delicious street food.

Practical Information:

Date: Bastille Day is celebrated on July 14th every year.

Cost: Most street events are free, but consider reserving a table at a beachside restaurant for an optimal view of the fireworks. Costs may range from $50 to $200.

Tips: Arrive early for the parade to secure a good viewing spot, and bring a picnic to enjoy on the beach before the fireworks begin.

Fête de la Musique (Music Day)

Join the global celebration of music during Fête de la Musique on June 21st. Nice comes alive with the sounds of various genres, from classical to contemporary, as musicians of all levels take to the streets, parks, and squares for impromptu performances.

Dive into the Melodic Melting Pot:

Street Performances: Wander through the Old Town and Promenade areas to discover an array of street musicians, bands, and soloists showcasing their talents. From jazz quartets to indie rock duos, the city becomes a symphony of diverse musical expressions.

Open-Air Stages: Seek out the designated open-air stages where professional and amateur musicians come together for larger performances. Place Garibaldi and Place Rossetti are popular locations featuring a variety of genres.

Community Participation: Embrace the participatory spirit by bringing your own instrument or joining a local jam session. The Fête de la Musique is a celebration of music for everyone.

Practical Information:

Date: Fête de la Musique takes place annually on June 21st, coinciding with the summer solstice.

Cost: Most street performances are free. Consider purchasing a drink or snack from nearby establishments to support local businesses.

Tips: Plan your route in advance to catch a variety of musical acts, and don't be afraid to interact with the performers.

Ironman Nice

For the athletic enthusiasts, witness the Ironman Nice, an exhilarating triathlon that takes place every summer. Athletes from around the world converge on the French Riviera to swim, bike, and run through the stunning landscapes of Nice.

Triumph of Endurance:

Swim in the Mediterranean: The race kicks off with a 2.4-mile swim in the azure waters of the Mediterranean Sea, providing a breathtaking start to the competition.

Scenic Bike Course: Cheer on the participants as they embark on a challenging 112-mile bike ride through picturesque coastal and mountainous terrain, including the famous Col de Vence.

Run Along the Promenade: The final leg takes athletes on a 26.2-mile run along the iconic Promenade des Anglais, with the cheering crowd providing the extra boost needed to reach the finish line.

Practical Information:

Date: Ironman Nice usually takes place in late June or early July. Check the official website for the current year's schedule.

Cost: Spectating is usually free, but if you're considering participating, entry fees for athletes range from $600 to $900.

Tips: Stake out spots along the route with the best views and bring snacks and refreshments to enjoy while watching the race.

Cannes Film Festival Excursion

While not hosted in Nice, the Cannes Film Festival in May is a glamorous and internationally renowned event that is a short distance away. Plan a day trip from Nice to experience the glitz and glamour of one of the most prestigious film festivals in the world.

A Day in the Film Industry Limelight:

Red Carpet Spectacle: Stroll along the famous Croisette and witness the spectacle of celebrities gracing the red carpet at the Palais des Festivals. Soak in the electric atmosphere as film premieres captivate audiences.

Cinematic Exploration: Take advantage of the numerous film screenings open to the public during the festival. Discover avant-garde works, international productions, and potentially catch a glimpse of your favorite stars.

Exclusive Events: If possible, attend exclusive parties and events surrounding the festival, immersing yourself in the glamour and sophistication of the cinematic world.

Practical Information:

Date: The Cannes Film Festival usually takes place in May. Check the official website for precise dates.

Cost: While attending public screenings can be relatively affordable, tickets to exclusive events and parties may range from $100 to $500 or more.

Tips: Plan your schedule around film screenings, and if attending premieres, arrive early to secure a good spot for celebrity sightings.

Christmas Markets in Nice

Experience the magic of the holiday season in Nice by exploring the enchanting Christmas markets that pop up across the city in December. The festive atmosphere, twinkling lights, and the aroma of mulled wine create a winter wonderland for locals and visitors alike.

Festive Delights and Seasonal Cheer:

Market Stalls: Wander through the various Christmas markets scattered across Nice, featuring stalls selling handmade crafts, ornaments, and local delicacies. Place Masséna and the Old Town are particularly festive.

Ice Skating: Enjoy the winter chill by lacing up your skates at the temporary ice rinks set up in the heart of the city. Skating under the Mediterranean sky is a unique and delightful experience.

Gastronomic Delights: Indulge in seasonal treats such as roasted chestnuts, gingerbread cookies, and mulled wine. The markets are a treasure trove of culinary delights perfect for the holiday season.

Practical Information:

Dates: Christmas markets in Nice usually open in early December and run until the end of the month.

Cost: Entrance to the markets is typically free, but bring some cash to indulge in festive treats and purchase unique gifts.

Tips: Visit the markets in the evening to experience the magical ambiance created by twinkling lights, and don't forget to try the local holiday specialties.

These annual highlights in Nice provide a diverse tapestry of experiences, showcasing the city's cultural richness, athletic prowess, cinematic allure, and festive charm. Whether you find yourself amidst the vibrant celebrations of Bastille Day or exploring the cinematic world of Cannes, each event adds a unique layer to the tapestry of Nice, ensuring that there's always something extraordinary happening in this Mediterranean paradise.

X. Conclusion

Final Thoughts on Nice

As the sun dips below the horizon, casting a warm glow over the azure waters of the Mediterranean, you find yourself lingering on the Promenade des Anglais, a place where the spirit of Nice truly comes alive. The palm-lined boulevard, stretching along the pebbly shores, is not just a promenade; it's a front-row seat to the magic of the French Riviera. As a local writer, I've had the privilege of immersing myself in the beauty and charm of Nice, and now, as you bid adieu to this captivating city, here are some final thoughts to carry with you.

1. The Riviera's Timeless Elegance

Nice embodies a timeless elegance that captivates every visitor. Whether you've explored the vibrant markets of Cours Saleya or meandered through the cobblestone streets of Old Town, you've likely sensed the fusion of history and modernity. The city's architecture, from the Baroque churches to the Belle Époque facades, weaves a narrative that transcends time. To truly grasp this elegance, consider joining a guided walking tour through the Old Town, where the past comes to life with every step.

2. Embrace the Culinary Tapestry

Nice is a haven for gastronomes, a place where the culinary scene dances between traditional Niçoise delicacies and innovative creations. Before you depart, indulge in a gastronomic journey that goes beyond the famous Niçoise Salad. Head to "La Merenda," a cozy eatery tucked away in Old Town, where you can savor authentic dishes like

Pissaladière and stockfish brandade. Remember, dining is an experience; embrace local flavors, and don't shy away from striking up a conversation with the chef.

3. Sunsets and Serenity

As the evening unfolds, seek serenity on Castle Hill, offering panoramic views of the city and the Mediterranean. It's not just about the destination; the journey matters too. Opt for a leisurely ascent, perhaps late in the afternoon, to witness the changing colors of the sky. Once at the top, find a quiet spot to revel in the spectacle of the sunset casting a warm glow over the city. The peaceful ambiance is a stark contrast to the vibrant energy found along the Promenade.

4. Cultural Immersion Beyond Museums

While the museums showcase the artistic prowess of Nice, cultural immersion extends beyond gallery walls. Attend local events and festivals, such as the renowned Nice Carnival or the Jazz Festival. Dive into the rhythm of the city; join locals in their joie de vivre. Visit the historic Opera de Nice for a dose of cultural performances that transcend language barriers.

Planning Your Next Visit

As you bid adieu to Nice, a city that has undoubtedly left an indelible mark on your heart, thoughts of a return journey begin to take shape. Planning your next visit is not just about ticking off missed attractions; it's about delving deeper into the essence of the Riviera. Here's a guide to help you plan your return, ensuring a seamless blend of familiar haunts and undiscovered gems.

1. Seasonal Delights and Timing

Nice's charm evolves with the seasons. While the summer months are synonymous with vibrant beach life and lively festivals, consider a return during the shoulder seasons of spring or fall. The weather remains pleasant, and you'll find a more relaxed atmosphere, allowing for a deeper connection with the city. Plan your visit around the Nice Carnival in February or the Jazz Festival in July for an extra layer of cultural richness.

2. Explore the Hinterland and Nearby Towns

Nice is not an isolated gem but a gateway to the picturesque hinterland and charming neighboring towns. Rent a car and explore the scenic landscapes of Provence or venture into the Alps-Maritimes. Discover the allure of Antibes, with its ancient ramparts, or the sophistication of Monaco. Each destination offers a unique perspective, providing a mosaic of experiences that complement Nice's coastal allure.

3. Dive Deeper into Local Cuisine

During your initial visit, you've scratched the surface of Niçoise cuisine. On your return, dive deeper. Take a cooking class to master the art of preparing Socca or explore the local markets to gather fresh ingredients for a homemade Ratatouille. Venture beyond the mainstream restaurants, seeking out hidden gems frequented by locals. Allow your taste buds to navigate the culinary labyrinth of Nice.

4. Connect with Locals

The heart of any city lies in its people. Plan your return with a focus on connecting with locals. Attend community events, participate in language exchange meet-ups, or simply strike up conversations at neighborhood cafés. This human interaction will unveil facets of Nice that guidebooks can't capture. Engage with the locals, and you'll find yourself welcomed into the vibrant tapestry of the city.

As you embark on planning your next visit, let the memories of vibrant markets, golden sunsets, and the harmonious blend of past and present guide your choices. Nice is not just a destination; it's a living story, waiting to be explored anew with each return. Until then, carry the spirit of the French Riviera in your heart, and let the anticipation of your next rendezvous with Nice ignite your wanderlust.